"Why is my kid so angry all the time?"
"We just can't talk to each other."
"I don't like the crowd my teenager is hanging around with lately."
"He just sits in his room with the door closed."
"She won't do anything around the house."
"What about my kid and sex?"

———————————————

Do these complaints sound familiar? They should—if you have a teenager around the house. Unfortunately these words usually go hand-in-hand with feelings of frustration and hopelessness—on the parent's part. But don't give up or throw your arms up in despair! Help is only a page away. Read on....

THE NINE MOST TROUBLESOME TEENAGE PROBLEMS

AND HOW TO SOLVE THEM

Lawrence Bauman, Ph. D., with Robert Riche

BALLANTINE BOOKS • NEW YORK

Library of Congress Catalog Card Number: 86-3814

ISBN 0-345-34290-9

This edition published by arrangement with Lyle Stuart Inc.

Manufactured in the United States of America

First Ballantine Books Edition: August 1987

To Pierre, 16, who was the ultimate inspiration for this book

Acknowledgments

Writing a book and keeping up with responsibilities at Coney Island Hospital, as well as carrying on a private practice of therapy with teen-agers and their families, has been more taxing than I had originally thought it would be when this book was begun. Fortunately, I had Robert Riche to share the work with me. His felicitous prose, as well as his practical and commonsense experience as a father of two teen-age children, were a great help in enabling me to make clear in a simple and direct way my particular approach in assisting parents with teen-agers who have problems. I am grateful to Bob. From beginning to end it was a pleasure and enriching experience working with him.

I am particularly grateful to my wife Josee who has encouraged me in the process of writing this book, and who has shown understanding and patience beyond the call of duty during the many late work nights and frequent work weekends during the many months that the book was being completed. I owe my son, Alexandre, and my daughter, Mia, a debt of gratitude, as well, for allowing me the privacy and space required to work when otherwise I might have been spending the time pleasurably in their company.

Special thanks to Karen De Grauw, who assisted in the gathering of information.

And, finally, I wish to acknowledge the important moral support of two people who encouraged me and were an inspiration in the early stages of the preparation of the book. To Lieselott Suares and Sara Matz I owe much, and in memory of them, I thank them.

L.B.

Contents

For Every Problem There's a Solution

Once upon a time there was a beautiful, loving, considerate and cheerfully obedient little child. The child was the apple of Daddy's eye, and a joy for Mommy to behold. Teachers at the school where the child attended sent back glowing reports of scholastic progress and successful social integration. The family frequently did wonderful things together, sometimes going on hikes and camping trips, or playing games on the front lawn; at other times, visiting museums and restaurants; occasionally finding pleasure in things as simple as just lolling about on the living room floor with the Sunday comics on sunny winter mornings.

Then, one day not long after the family had celebrated the child's thirteenth birthday, a darkening mood made its presence felt in the household. Certain physical changes began to occur in the child which made the child feel awkward and unattractive, resulting in a moodiness that was directed toward others. The child was not quite as considerate as previously, and when this was pointed out to the child by the parents, the child seemed to resent the criticism, and to withdraw into a shell.

The parents, considering themselves to be reasonably enlightened, at first accepted the changes with a certain rueful curiosity, hoping that in time the child would become happy and cheerful again. But, in fact, as time went on, the child seemed to become less and less happy and cheerful, and in fact, there were times when the child's moody presence cast a gloom over the lives of the entire family.

Nothing seemed to work to bring the child back. Neither kindness, nor entreaties, nor scolding, nor withholding of privileges, nor outright punishment. In fact, the more the parents tried to bring the child around the more the child responded in a disagreeable manner. As surprised as they were, and as reluctant to admit it, the parents began to realize that their child didn't confide in them any more. The child resented any advice, sometimes refusing even to listen. It appeared, moreover, that the child didn't like them anymore, maybe even had *contempt* for them. The child's grades began to slip; there was a suspicion that maybe the child was experimenting with drugs and alcohol; when confronted with these suspicions, the child refused to be candid. The child began to hang out with a bad crowd.

The fact is that the beautiful, loving, considerate and cheerfully obedient little child quite suddenly had become transformed, metamorphosed, into an unattractive, surly, inconsiderate and tyrannical *stranger* in the house. Most distressing of all, no matter what the parents tried to do, the situation seemed to deteriorate day by day.

"What happened to our beautiful child?" the parents asked themselves. "Did we do something wrong along the way?" "How could something like this happen—to us?" "Where will it all end?"

The parents felt helpless, confused, frightened, even to the point of panic, that their beautiful, loving, considerate and cheerfully obedient child was turning into a slovenly, dishonest, under-achieving, disobedient, undisciplined and irresponsible PUNK KID! The prognosis: The kid was on its way to ending up as a dropout from society, a parasite, a drug addict, a CRIMINAL, a jailbird, a MURDERER!

This is the kind of fearful complaint I hear every working day of my life from parents with teen-age boys and girls. They come to me for advice on how to bring back the joy and happiness into their homes that seems now to have flown away forever. These parents—and their children, let us not forget—are really suffering. There is nothing amusing or funny about the misery of escorting a young troubled child through the teen-age years to young adulthood. It is often a painful, bitter, frustrating, despairing and, worst of all, terrifying experience. Suddenly it seems to the parents that all of their previous education and training, their common sense, their goodwill, their basic decency, their sense of humor, their unselfish desire to give their children as many opportunities as possible counts for nothing—nothing works. They are getting nowhere. They have worked sensibly and conscientiously for the first thirteen years to make it possible for their beautiful child to grow into a beautiful adult, and this *creature* that confronts them suddenly, whom they love more than anything else in the world, is turning before their eyes into a *monster*. They are in an absolute panic and in despair. They feel their own lives have been a *failure*, and they don't know which way to turn. For the fact is, NOBODY HAS EVER TOLD THEM HOW TO RAISE A TEEN-AGE KID. They simply are not prepared and so do not know how to deal with what they are suddenly confronted with.

Over the past eight years I have worked with more than 100 teen-age boys and girls and their parents, and it has been during that time that I have come to realize that although every single case study is in certain respects unique, there are at the same time common threads that run through all relationships between teen-agers and their parents. With that realization in mind, it has occurred to me that it would serve a purpose simply to spell out some of these recognizable common denominators and suggest some approaches to solving problem situations that have worked for the teen-age kids and their families that I have seen. Hence, this book which, by and large, attempts to provide you, the parent, with everything you ever wanted to know about raising your teen-age kid.

Yes, there really are common threads running between parent-teen-age problem relationships. Does that surprise anyone? Ask any of your neighbors or friends with teen-age kids of their own. Okay, you already have. And what is your conclusion? It's the same story over and over again: The horrors of the teen-age years. You can spend a whole social evening discussing with your friends the trials and tribulations of your teen-age kids. And *you have done this.* And why? Because there is a recognizable common denominator running through all of your experiences, and it's reassuring to know that you are not alone.

Still, you say, knowing that others have problems doesn't remove yours. And you're right about that. But be reassured, with a bit of calmness and common sense, and a few helpful hints, your kids will grow up to healthy adulthood. Because, believe it or not, the vast majority of kids still do grow up and become responsible members of society, just as you did, even though you, too, may very likely have been, in case you've forgotten, a teen-age horror once yourself.*

The Teen-Age Years

What is the matter with kids today? I hear this question asked more than any other. Why are kids so rebellious? So discourteous? So bored with themselves and disinterested in life? All they want to do, it seems, is to hang out with a bad crowd and listen to crazy music.

Let me call something to your attention. Kids have *always* been rebellious, to one degree or another. They have always been rebellious and discourteous, at times. They have always been

---

*I think it is important to point out at this point—without attempting to raise any additional alarming fears—that in some few cases changes in emotional behavior during the teen-age years can be a signal of underlying physical problems. I advocate as a general rule that all teen-agers be given periodic thorough physical examinations by the family doctor, at which time any unusual emotional behavior should be discussed with the examining physician.

disinterested and bored and wondering what to do with themselves.

Remember when *you* were a teen-ager? Try to remember. How about those fights with Dad over the car? Mom complaining that you never helped anymore around the house. Dad telling you to turn down that radio. Was there trouble at home about smoking cigarettes? Did you ever *lie* to your parents? Did you ever sneak off to some place you were told specifically not to go to? The conflict between parents and their teen-age children is documented throughout history.

Have you ever heard of an *Oedipus complex*? It is based on the legendary Greek king Oedipus who unwittingly killed his father and married his mother. It was his *fate*. I am not suggesting that this is the fate of *your* family, but many of the *concerns* of the ancient Greeks with reference to the relationship between fathers and sons are the *same kinds* of concerns we have today.

In Shakespeare's *King Lear*, the old king disinherits his most loving daughter, Cordelia, simply because she refuses to flatter him falsely. The tragic consequence is that he is driven mad by his own sorrow and guilt. Turgenev, the great 19th-century Russian novelist, dealt in *Fathers and Sons* with the conflicts between generations and changing times. (Does the phrase, "Times are different today" sound familiar to anyone?) D.H. Lawrence in *Sons and Lovers* documented the struggles of a son to break free of the hold his mother has on him.

Yes, you say, maybe there has always been conflict, but things are worse today than ever before. It is just possible they really are more difficult. But before we look into that, let's just take a look at what it is like to be a teen-ager.

The myth of teen-age kids as being like Andy Hardy or the kids on the television show "Happy Days" is just that—a myth. Sure, those shows have captured some of the humor and eccentric behavior of teen-age kids. But what they don't reveal is the underlying fear and uncertainty and frustration that exist in teen-age kids as well. For teen-agers, too, are in a situation where *nobody has ever told them everything they ought to know about growing up.* And if somebody ever did try to tell them, they probably wouldn't listen, anyway, because that's part of growing up—the process of learning to think for themselves and not do what they are advised to do by others who are older and have been telling them what to do for the first dozen years of their lives.

Teen-agers are going through rapid and drastic changes. Suddenly they sense being on a wild ride, in a vehicle they don't know how to operate, on a trip to they are not quite sure where. All they know is that their situation is serious, and that nobody else (especially an adult) can quite appreciate the situation enough to help them. They feel that they must work out of it *on their own*, and bring the vehicle under control and journey into focus.

And they are right! In the long run, they must take control of their own lives, and that is what they are in the process of trying to do, if we will let them. If we want to help them, we must approach them very carefully.

The vehicle they are riding in is a human body. Suddenly these bodies are out of control. Zits (pimples), are breaking out for no good reason on their

faces. Hair is springing out from all kinds of places.
Girls are suddenly experiencing the monthly occur-
rence of menstruation and the growth and enlargement (and sometimes not quite enough, or too much,
enlargement to suit them) of their breasts. Boys are
experiencing changes in their voices so that they
don't even sound like themselves, and the exquisite
but not quite acceptable experience of sexual
dreams.

And all of these physical changes signal that it's
time for new ways of relating to the real world out
there. Teen-agers can no longer expect Mommy and
Daddy to live their lives for them. Nor do they want
them to. They feel this instinctively. And now they
are casting about to form new behavior patterns of
their own. Watch them as they flail their arms about
in awkward gestures, as if frantically trying to
break free of the old constraints while at the same
time trying to grasp onto a whirling adult world
that isn't quite ready to accept them yet.

In the course of this process of change, teen-agers
often are as frightened as you are. They think nobody else—certainly not their parents—has ever
been so unsure of themselves as *they* are. Nobody
understands what they are going through, they
think. Their parents' suggestions are "ridiculous."
Because the way that their parents solved their own
teen-age metamorphosis, for the most part, won't
work to solve the problem today in a new social context. For example, Mom in a mini-skirt as she tries
to be a "pal" to her teen-age daughter often finds
that she is more of an embarrassment, because in
the daughter's eyes mothers just don't know what
it's like to win the attention of the local rock band

lead singer. (After all, she married "old reliable" Dad, didn't she?)

Because they feel that no adult can understand, and because they are afraid to expose their inner-most confusions to people who do not and cannot understand, teen-agers tend to become secretive (because they are fearful of ridicule); irritable (because they resent interference from those who can't really understand); boastful (because by blustering, maybe it will fool others into thinking they are in charge of themselves, or maybe even convince themselves that they are in charge); depressed (because much of the time nothing seems to work out right); rebel-lious (because parents always seem to have a rule that either interferes with their rocky lives, or does not apply); defiant (because that's the only way they know to get the parents to leave them alone), and even devious (because direct confrontation is too un-pleasant and may cause more pain in the short run than they believe is tolerable).

This is the pattern of the typical American family with teen-age kids today. Mom and Dad "can't do anything with them." The kids are secretive, irrit-able, boastful, depressed, rebellious, defiant and even devious.

Is it worse today than ever before? In my opinion, there is some reason to believe that it may be. Al-though the rite of passage has always been difficult, specific aspects of our society *have changed*, result-ing in some new and unique problems that put a great strain on teen-agers today. Certainly the *op-tions* open to teen-agers are greater than at any time in previous history, giving them choices to deal with and decisions to make that they are not experienced enough to deal with. For example, just 25 years ago only a few kids went "all the way" with the opposite sex. Today sexual intercourse is more widely accepted among teen-agers. To illustrate how far sexual awareness has come over the past two decades, you have only to compare the difference in the "health education" courses of the 60's and the "sex education" courses of today. Where there used to be schematic drawings of male and female reproductive organs, and very little further mention of the subject, today the focus is on contraception, abortion, family planning, incest and sexual abuse. In many circles, sexual intercourse among teen-agers today is not only accepted, but *expected*. There is a new freedom, but with that freedom there are new pressures to perform, even though one may not be inclined to do so.

Certainly drugs are more available today than they were 25 years ago. Many kids today have been exposed to the fact of drug trafficking even before they have left elementary school. The temptation to show off or be "one of the crowd" puts enormous pressure on today's teen-agers. Drugs simply are another contemporary youthful "fad," but unlike fads of previous generations, the new one can lead to erosion of the work ethic, to physical deterioration, and worse, to death by overdose or vehicular accident.

Quite apart from the matters of sexual freedom and drug availability, the world itself seems to become a more frightening place every year, as the superpower nations build up their stocks of nuclear weapons and other doomsday devices, and efforts to accommodate peacefully to the nuclear age do not seem to succeed. This pervasive threat of doom cannot help but exert an underlying dispiriting influence, causing teen-age kids (as well as adults) to wonder whether in the face of world destruction it's worth making the effort to be a responsible citizen.*

Also, you've heard it said a million times that we are a youth-oriented society. What this means is nothing more than that there is a great consumer market out there among teen-agers, and the people with things to sell aren't forgetting it for one minute. Our society spends billions of dollars in aiming its messages at teenagers, whether it be movies designed to get them to come back six times (paying upwards of $4 each time) or buying new skin preparations to get rid of zits. The barrage of messages to the effect that teen-age life should be unadulterated carefree joy (if they buy the right products), at a time in their lives when they are unable to be carefree about anything because they are too busy trying to figure out where they fit in, probably succeeds more than anything else in making them have even more doubts about themselves.

So, yes, we can all probably agree that teen-agers do have a lot of problems these days—problems brought on by the mere fact that they are teen-agers going through the changes that teen-agers have gone through since the beginning of the history of man—aggravated by the fact that these are fast times, precarious times, even cynical times.

And, yes, as a result of the many aggravated problems that teen-agers have today, their parents are faced with aggravated difficulties in trying to help their kids through their teen-age years. Let's

---

*Even though during the teen-age years of many of today's parents there was the Vietnam War, there was at that time, as distinct, in my opinion, from today, a feeling that something could be done, as so often now there does not seem to be.

face it, no matter *what* you expected, you never expected that things would be as difficult as they have turned out to be. As one father said to me recently, "This kid has problems, all right, but he's driving me and his mother absolutely crazy!"

How to Cope

My job, in essence, is to help teen-age youngsters get through and over some of the rough spots of their teen-age years as constructively as possible. While I am doing this I also help their parents get over the fears and anxieties and feelings of helplessness that they are experiencing as their children manifest what seems to them to be irrational, anti-social, and unacceptable behavior. When I consult with a family that comes to me for help, I don't whip any magic formulas out of my sleeve. We talk, and we try to reach a common understanding of the problem, and then the family goes home and tries to work out solutions in the arena of real life. Because I am in a position to observe recognizable common denominators in the kinds of problems that come up, oftentimes I am able to make suggestions that turn out to be helpful. I think of myself not so much as a "doctor treating patients" or "analysands," if you prefer, but as a *facilitator* who points out possible solutions to problems which the family can try out after they leave my office as they go about living their everyday lives.

So, too, will this book attempt to *facilitate* your efforts to solve some of the problems that you have with your teen-age kids. It will provide you with examples of people who have problems that you will recognize as being like your own, and it will offer suggestions as to how you can work on those problems and turn them around.

As a starting point, the most valuable general observation that has presented itself to me in working with the families that have come to my office is that 99 times out of a hundred *a kid with problems is not a kid who is abnormal.* This is important for you to realize, for the way you think about your kid can have a profound effect on how your kid develops.

Teen-agers with problems, for the most part, are not "patients." Problems are a very normal part of teen-age growing up. The single most important thing you can do as a caring parent to help your troubled kid solve some of his or her teen-age problems is to stop worrying about whether the kid is "normal" or "abnormal" and begin to try to understand better what's bothering him (her).

Oh, sure, you say. But *how?* You've been trying your darndest up to now, and you haven't succeeded, which is why you are practically out of your mind and willing to delve into the pages of this book. *Relax.* By the time you have finished reading and have observed the common threads that run through the problems of all teen-agers today you should have sufficient new insights to enable you to understand better than you ever have before the various problems of your teen-age kids.

But *understanding is just the first step.* The hard part is *acting* on the basis of understanding—acting in a way that will help your teen-age kid and yourself. How should you act? We will see various solutions to specific problem areas as we go along, but in every case *the solution will depend to a large ex-*

*tent on the parents' willingness to change in accord-
ance with the changes of their teen-age kids.*

Yes, *you* must change. The key to helping your
teen-age kid into developing constructively into a
responsible young adult depends upon you, first, understanding what is going on, and then, second,
*changing the way you behave and react in relation
to your kid.*

What I am saying here is that *there is never to be
a return of that beautiful, loving, considerate and
cheerfully obedient child you used to know.* That's
right! And the sooner you stop trying to push for it,
to insist on it, the sooner you will allow him or her
to develop into a reasonable young adult. The new
identity of your young adult offspring may very well
turn out to be beautiful, loving, considerate and
cheerful, even obedient, but it will show itself in
new ways that only by your own growth and change
will you be able to recognize.

The theme of this book is that the key to helping
your youngster over the problems of his or her teen-
age years is that *you change—first.* You have to take
the first step. And that step will be hard. It may
mean giving up many cherished notions of "how
children ought to be raised." You've got to throw
away some of those old ideas you hold, and begin to
deal with your teen-ager the way he or she really
is, and not the way you think they ought to be. Take,
for example, the old idea of "children should be seen
but not heard." Can you imagine anything more out
of date? Does anyone today really think he can separate teen-agers from the loud music that is so much
an important part of their lives?

Instead of invariably and inflexibly reacting to
behavior of your teen-ager that you disapprove of

you must begin to look for the underlying cause for that behavior. In almost every case, a "bad" kid is signalling a legitimate grievance that he or she does not know how to express any other way. It is through your understanding of what that teen-ager is signalling, and then by your effort to change yourself sufficiently to be able to respond to it—not as a "parent to a little kid," but as a caring older adult to a younger adult—that you will serve your own and your teen-ager's best purpose.

Let me give an example: A 15-year-old boy was brought in to see me by his parents because they felt he was slipping away into antisocial behavior. Although he was average or slightly above average in intelligence, he was doing badly in his grades at school, actually flunking one course, and getting D's in others. He had been suspended once for a week when he was caught smoking marijuana in a closet with another boy. He was beginning to "hang out" with a group of slightly older kids at the town parking lot—kids who also were having trouble in school and were rumored to be smoking marijuana and drinking beer in the afternoons. The boy began to develop slovenly habits, and he insisted on hand-painting on his jackets a variety of death's heads and snakes and other hideous creatures. (Rather well-done renderings, incidentally.) All he ever seemed to want to do was to lie about and listen to loud rock music and read motorcycle magazines.

The parents were concerned, and wondered if I could help their son. The first thing I did was arrange a schedule of meetings the parents and the boy would attend together. If the key to smoothing the passage from childhood to young adulthood through the teen-age years is the ability of parents to understand and to change in accordance with the new personalities of their children then it often is helpful for the parents to be present to participate in what is going on, and then work out satisfactory ways of changing their approach. I try to have the first meeting with parents in the presence of the teen-agers. (Exceptions are made in some instances.)

The parents of this particular boy were reasonably sensitive to their son's suffering, but they didn't know what to do, and they were suffering on their own. (Perhaps they were aware of their own suffering before they came to realize that their son was suffering, too.) The boy was not very communicative at first, though he was willing to come to the sessions.

His parents didn't understand him, the boy said. They placed too many restrictions on him. He was given too many household chores. His life was boring. All familiar complaints of teen-agers.

Early on in our talks the father finally asked the boy what he could do that would please his son the most. The boy replied. "Let me have a dirt-track motorcycle" (this is a lightweight motorcycle built for riding cross country, not for the street).

The father's first reaction was "never in a million years!" To him, as we found out later, a motorcycle was a metaphor for Hell's Angels and the kind of crowd that his son was already hanging out with at the parking lot.

Later, recognizing the importance of at least putting up the pretense of "being reasonable," the father did relent to the extent of telling his son that if he got all A's in school he could have the motorcycle. This was his initial way of "changing" to relate better to his young son. He claimed that he was being "fair" by making the offer. Of course, deep down he knew, as the rest of us did, that it would be many years before the boy would be able to bring his grades up to all A's. He figured that by the time the boy got his grades up to a point where he could have the motorcycle he would have outgrown the desire for it. The father was pretty pleased with himself for his cleverness.

The son, of course, without ever having heard his father admit to his reasoning, intuitively knew better than any of us that this was his father's manipulative way of thinking. The son's way of fighting back, as it gradually became pieced together, was simply to *act out all the horror fantasies of a "biker" that his father wouldn't let him be*.

It was at this point that I suggested that perhaps if the boy could bring his one flunking grade up to passing that would be a start. In return for that effort the father might then consider giving the boy a motorcycle, and we could observe where that led. The father, with a little urging from the mother, finally agreed to the bargain. (Probably because everything else had failed.)

In the very next marking period the boy managed to get a C in the subject that he had been flunking, and the father was obliged to let him have a dirt-track motorcycle. (They went 50/50 on the cost.)

"Buying him that bike was the best thing I ever did," the father said later. Having wanted the motorcycle for several years, the boy took care of it with loving affection, tuning it, cleaning it, beginning to read about internal combustion engines. He had very little time for "hanging out" at the parking lot. He was too busy riding his motorcycle through the woods in the town. He began to clear extra trails (after first getting permission to do so) and began to take some interest in trail clearing and general outdoorsmanship. At the same time, he began to share some of his enthusiasms with the family, as he had not before. His grades in school continued to improve. After riding his motorcycle, he would shower and clean up, taking a greater interest in his appearance. In short, having been treated, for a change, as a responsible person, he began to act more like one.

The parents, being, as I said, sensitive people, recognized immediately the improvement that was going on, and responded by allowing their son to have other privileges that he previously had been denied. They stopped interrogating him, for example, about his every movement out of their sight. As they began to trust the young man more, he began to take on more responsibility for himself. And that family was on the road to becoming one in which the family members felt close again. When problems would come up—as long as there was a recognition by both sides that there was no manipulation going on, but simply a willingness to negotiate and to understand and to compromise—the family was able to solve them.

The situation with this family illustrates the point that I am making—that during the teen-age passage families must change their ways of looking at one another. And the process must start by the parents taking the first steps. A *new creature is developing* who is as different as a butterfly from the caterpillar. Really! Between the caterpillar and the butterfly are the chrysalis years in the cocoon. This is the period of the teen-age years, and this is when the real change takes place. The teen-ager *is going to change*, because nature insists upon it. The child is developing *an adult identity*. If you as parents want to help make that process as smooth as possible you have to do some changing of your own. Believe me, it will pay dividends in the long run.

Not only will you end up with a happier teen-ager, one who finds his or her own identity with less pain, but as that identity forms, the teen-ager may even begin to recognize that *you have an identity, too*! You are not just Mom and Dad. You are people with identities of your own. Okay, so maybe you're a *little weird* at first, but as they begin to realize that you are not just authority figures, but reasonable people who respect the changes that have occurred in *them*, they will respond by beginning to treat *you* with respect, as well. Yes! You do not have to *force* them to respect you. It won't work, in any event. You have to *earn* their respect by, first, understanding and then, second, accommodating to the changes that have taken place in them as a result of their emerging new identities.

What About Rules?

Does understanding and accommodating to the changes that are taking place in your teen-ager mean you should *give in* to every teen-age whim, no matter how ridiculous or destructive? Certainly not! Are there to be *no rules* for teen-agers that must be obeyed? Of course there are rules that must be obeyed! Is Dr. Bauman advocating total permissiveness? No, Dr. Bauman is not advocating total permissiveness! Won't all of this understanding and accommodating lead to *teen-age tyranny* in the home?

No. What I am advocating will not lead to teenage tyranny in the home. As a matter of fact, it is precisely to escape tyranny of the teen-agers that we want to solve the family's problems. Yes, teenagers can be tyrannical. But tyranny takes many forms. Even if you should succeed in forcing a rebellious teen-ager to obey every rule you lay down, the youngster has ways of working his or her tyranny over the entire family. Is there any tyranny worse than living in a house in which a teen-ager permits no joy, no satisfaction, no sharing of life's mutual pleasures? Instead, the house is filled with misery, gloom, despair, even hatred. A teen-ager who is forced to obey every rule can nonetheless inflict a tyranny of hell on a family. You, the parent, may win every single battle over your teen-age youngster, but you are losing the total war—and you know it. Your end desire is peace and love, but if you insist on acting as a jailer instead of an understanding parent, you simply will create more resentment, and watch peace and love become a more and more remote possibility.

Yes, *it is important to have rules, and that those rules be obeyed.* No family can exist together in a home unless there are rules that are obeyed. Neither can society as a whole function without rules. Nations of the world must have rules. But rules sometimes have to be bent to changing times and circumstances.

And *not all rules should be made up by parents.* Democracy is a concept we all pay lip service to, but as parents, we sometimes neglect to live by democratic rules in the home. When your beautiful obedient child was young, there was no need for democracy. You, as a loving parent, were able to rule by means of a benevolent dictatorship. But this changing creature in your home now has ideas of his or her own, and some of the rules that you think are best for the child may be just a little bit out of touch with the reality of your changing teen-ager. Rules previously established have to be pushed and squeezed and accommodated a little bit to take in the desires of the family as a whole.

It may surprise you, but the fact of the matter is that *teen-age kids actually want rules*. I have never— repeat, never—found a kid to tell me that he didn't want any rules at all. *Less* rules, maybe. But never no rules. We all live by rules. Rules enable us to see how well we're doing in life. We measure ourselves against rules. If you do such-and-such, you will achieve this-and-that. That's the way the world works. If you drive on the right side of the road (in the U.S.A.), you will not run into oncoming traffic. Rules can be very satisfying. They give a sense of security, which teen-agers need most of all. It is only when rules seem oppressive that we try to break them.

Let's look back for a minute at the family with the teen-ager who wanted the motorcycle. Did the family, in fact, give in to the tyranny of the boy? Well, the father against his own first instinct did break down and let the boy have a motorcycle. But the boy did bring his flunking grade up to a C. Once the parent was able to understand that the teen-ager's desire for a motorcycle had to be taken seriously as a step in his growing up, as a way of the son to test his ability with a machine, with the responsibility of caring for it, then the teen-ager began to do his part. And the spiral went upward from there. The boy, for his part, began to take a different attitude toward himself and toward his parents.

What were the rules in this instance? And what rules were broken or bent? The first rule was that the teen-ager should do his homework, pay attention in class, and not flunk out of school. That rule was *obeyed*. The son was then permitted to have his motorcycle.

Once the motorcycle was allowed, it set up the need for new sets of rules: Who would pay for the gas? If the teen-age son didn't neglect his chores (emptying the garbage, mowing the lawn), the father would see to it that maintenance costs of the motorcycle were met.

And thus, the family was cooperating to everyone's mutual interest—a lesson in growing up that was not lost on the teen-ager, nor on the parents, either.

Instead of permissiveness, I call this kind of solving of problems a *creative synthesis*. If you 1) succeed in understanding your teenager's particular needs, and 2) accommodate your life and adjust your family rules to the changing situation, you will arrive at a creative synthesis wherein you bring together the separate elements of thought within the family into a unified view. You will have won reasonable—repeat, *reasonable*—concessions from your teen-ager, and you will have undergone an inner growth in understanding on your own part. This is not permissiveness. This is a creative synthesis within a family.

I'd like to give another example of a creative synthesis that I observed recently that illustrates understanding by the parents and a willingness to bend and change (by both the parents and the teen-ager) that solved a problem that is very common and that you may recognize.

I was working with a 16-year-old girl and her family. The girl was attractive, normally obedient, but feeling that she should be allowed to stay out at night as late as she wanted. The family came to see me because they were worried about the girl's growing independence (can you imagine!), and a growing tendency on her part to be irritable, disagreeable, "unhappy," and an unwillingness to talk to the parents about what was bothering her.

"I'm not doing anything wrong when I go out at night," the girl complained to me. And as near as I could tell, it was true, she was not doing anything "wrong." She and some of her high school friends, mostly girls, would go to the local bowling alley where pizzas and Cokes were served, and they would sit there for an evening, and meet and talk with their friends, both male and female. Quite innocent. Nevertheless, the idea of a young teen-age girl staying out to all hours of the night was unacceptable to this particular family, and so the family had fixed a curfew of 11 P.M. on week-end nights. Although the girl obeyed the curfew, there was a continuing series of arguments about extending the curfew to a later hour.

One week-end night the girl didn't return until one A.M. The mother and father retaliated by immediately "grounding" their daughter for a two-week period.

When the following week-end arrived the daughter was reminded that she was "grounded" and could not go out to the bowling alley. This created a terrific scene, the girl insisting that an 11 P.M.

curfew was too early, and that she should be allowed to go out again this week-end and to stay out until at least one A.M.

The mother would not discuss changing the curfew, and insisted that the "grounding" had nothing to do with the hour of the curfew, anyway. Rather, it had to do with the fact that the daughter had disobeyed and broken a pre-existing and "agreed upon" rule. The daughter became defiant at this point, insisting that she was going to go out anyway, regardless of what her mother wanted. The mother replied that if the daughter went out she shouldn't plan on coming back, because the door would be locked against her.

Both sides were in a non-compromising confrontational situation which was escalating. The daughter was being forced into defying her mother and staying out all night, just to save face. The mother could not back down on her insistence that the daughter was "grounded." At this point, fortunately, the father stepped in, taking the part of intermediary, or referee. He talked with his daughter alone for more than an hour, and the daughter spilled out all of her complaints. The family didn't trust her. They didn't realize that she was only asking for the same rights that all the other kids had, etc., etc. After listening to her arguments, the father (following a brief consultation with the mother, who was only too happy to have a compromise solution) agreed with the daughter that perhaps she was right, that an 11 P.M. curfew on week-ends was too early. He asked the daughter if she would accept a 12 midnight curfew. The daughter readily agreed. (She, too, was happy to have a compromise solution.) The father then pointed out that the "grounding" was in response to the breaking of a rule, and that the rules of the house had to be followed. Therefore, he proposed a deal: If the daughter would accept her "punishment" and not go out on this particular night, the father and mother would rescind the "grounding" for the following week-end. Having won the right to stay out until midnight (which everyone later agreed was reasonable in terms of the standards of the town set by the girl's peers), the daughter was willing to accept her "punishment" for having broken the previous curfew rule (even though perhaps the rule had not been enlightened).

After that, the girl was permitted to stay out until 12, though just as often as not she was home by 11:30, or even 11. But her parents had allowed her to win an important right. She had become a contributor in setting the household rules. In point of fact, she had been treated as an adult, and responded by acting responsibly, first, by not defying her mother and going out when she was "grounded," and secondly, by obeying the new curfew hour to the letter in months to follow. The incident and its solution marked the beginning of a re-examination of the whole relationship wherein the parents had been unwilling to acknowledge that their "little girl" was suddenly growing up.

A creative synthesis of the various seemingly unalterably opposed points of view won out over unyielding discipline. The parents had recognized that their young daughter was a bit older and had more rights than they at first had been willing to permit. They also had accommodated, changed their own way of looking at their daughter, which was a signal to the daughter that she was being treated as

an adult, with the result that she responded by acting in an adult fashion. A destructive confrontation
was avoided, and the family was able to go about
its daily associations in a more positive manner.

Coming to the synthesis of ideas, I do not believe,
is the same as being permissive. The world works
in the same kind of way. Couples who stay together
come to an eventual synthesis of ideas. (This does
not mean that they always agree on every point;
sometimes it can mean that they agree to disagree.
Which is just as good, if both sides agree to it.) Nations negotiate their disagreements similarly. If
they don't, the world cannot survive. Is there any
better lesson a teen-ager could learn about the world
than that the most locked-in positions between the
members of a family can be negotiated successfully
if there is willingness to appreciate the other's point
of view?

I would like to put in at this point *a word of caution* having to do with the process of reaching a synthesis of thought in a family problem situation. The
word of caution is this: Reaching a synthesis does
not necessarily and invariably mean that in every
dealing with our teen-agers we should talk every
problem to death. Sometimes there can be such a
thing as *too much talking.* Parents, who usually are
better talkers, tend to use talk as a way of manip-
ulating their teen-agers into following old rules that
applied when they were younger. *Talk can be a way
of resisting change.*

The father and mother of one family that I worked
with were very proud of the fact that whenever
there was a disagreement between the children and
the adults, they had always held a "family meeting" to talk things out. It turned out that the teen-

agers always came away from these "democratic meetings" having lost the argument. The parents didn't realize that the "meetings" they held were simply ways of enforcing their own views through the clever use of words.

Be careful! Be honest with yourself and your children. Talk out problems, by all means. But not all teen-agers, you should remember, want to talk, or are able at this stage in their lives to risk expressing all their innermost feelings, even when to do so might best serve everyone's purpose. In such cases, this is where your creativity comes into play. You have to "read between the lines," so to speak; you have to observe your teen-ager's unexpressed aspirations, and then accommodate to the new situation.

Sometimes you just have to recognize that your teen-ager needs *privacy*. He or she *doesn't want to talk*, even though they do desperately need *understanding*. Try to conduct yourself in such a way in these circumstances that you can indicate *non-verbally* that you do understand. Perhaps you can offer a privilege hitherto denied, and say nothing more. See how that works. Love is, as they say in the song, "a many splendored thing." By showing love through an act of a generous changed attitude, rather than just by talking about it, sometimes you can work miracles. Love, understanding, creativity—they are all connected. And sometimes just by showing these traits, by demonstrating them, with very little talk involved, you are able to express yourself in the most eloquent manner possible. People—even teen-agers—respond to love. You may be surprised at how much things can improve around the house.

What If Your Kid Won't Listen to Reason

Some kids, you may say, just simply won't respond to anything you do. Every effort to compromise on your part is taken as a sign of weakness that the teen-ager tries to take advantage of.

It is true, there are some instances of this kind, and I have worked with families with very difficult problems.* Usually, the worst problems between teen-agers and their parents are in those homes where the worst problems exist between the parents themselves. I have worked with families where the parents are divorced; in some cases, the problem is intensified because the divorced partners will not cooperate together for the good of their own children!

None of this changes the basic need for understanding by the parents and the need for them to change and accommodate to the changing personalities of their teen-agers. Broken families, too, can succeed in solving the problems they have with their children. It certainly can add to the problems of raising teen-agers if you are a single parent. Nonetheless, it usually presents less of a problem than if the husband and wife stay together in the face of very serious marital difficulties that create tension in the house.

Whatever the situation, the way to smooth the road is to take the time to understand what the underlying needs are of your teenager and then make

*If you find that after reading this book carefully and giving it a good try you cannot improve your family situation, you and your teen-ager may feel that you need professional assistance. At the end of the book there is a listing of social service agencies that you can call for referral guidance.

the accommodation that will best help that youngster cross over into young adulthood. It just takes a
bit more patience and understanding than you ever
thought you would have to have. But it's worth it!
Helping your teen-age youngster negotiate these difficult years is one of the greatest accomplishments
you will ever know in your life, and the effort will
be worth it when young adulthood finally arrives
and your offspring and you can look back and smile
on all the difficult trials and travails you had together over those few years.

Everything You Ever Wanted to Know About Raising Your Teen-age Kid

And so now we are ready to get down to the nitty
gritty of how to deal with the everyday problems
you face with your teen-age kid(s). This book is organized into nine sections, each one dealing with a
specific question that you probably would like to
know more about.

Each section is organized in a form that addresses
immediately the problems you have in your home
with your teen-age kid. The basic structure is very
simple and my intention is to be as realistic and
practical as possible.

First, *the title of each section* is in the form of a
common complaint, such as, "My Kid and I Can't
Talk to Each Other" (Problem #6). This is the statement of the problem that you would like solved.
Non-confiding is one of the common threads we
spoke of earlier that runs through all problems we
find among teen-agers. Why don't teen-agers want
to confide more in their parents?

Second, therefore, based on the family cases I have worked with, there is *a brief comment on the phenomenon*, in this example, that of teen-agers not confiding in their parents. This, in itself, oftentimes provides the understanding that we talked about earlier that you will be searching for. Understanding will enable you to begin grappling with the problem.

Third, we get into *some actual casebook examples*. (The identities of the families involved are protected.) The common thread, the recognizable common denominator, will begin to be seen. Not in every detail perhaps. But in the several examples I will give, you will see common traits.

Fourth, I will then show *the method that was brought to bear to solve the problems* of each particular family used as an example. Changes in attitude of the parents that succeeded in bringing about a common synthesis of ideas will be emphasized.

And, fifth, just so that we don't miss anything not included in the examples given, I'll offer some *summary suggestions* that you might try to work out with your teen-age kid.

Don't be surprised if some of the material in the different sections overlaps to some extent. Rarely are the problems of teen-agers—or anyone else, for that matter—totally isolated into separate categories. When a family comes to me with worries about their teen-age kid's failing grades in school it usually is not long before we are talking about who the teen-age youngster hangs out with, what job duties and responsibilities he or she has been given around the house, how much do the parents and teen-ager trust each other, etc., etc. This discussion continues until we have formed a clearer understanding of this particular family's problems, and then can set about attacking specific problems—including the original problem of failing grades.

You will note that up to this point I have for the most part referred to teen-age boys and girls simply as "teen-agers," without making any special differentiation between the sexes. I have done this deliberately, for, in my experience, many, if not most, of the problems of teen-age boys and girls are identical—at least, insofar as their relationships with their parents are concerned. For example, it doesn't make very much difference whether the teen-ager is a boy or a girl when it comes to the complaint that parents so often have: "My Kid Won't Take on Responsibility." (Problem #1.)

Nevertheless, it certainly is true that both girls and boys do have special problems that pertain to their different sexes, and in the course of this book, I will make reference to their special concerns. (Note particularly Problem #9: "What About My Kid and Sex?")

So, now, let's get to work. If you like, you can jump right into the section dealing with the problem that most interests you. Or you can take each section in order. Either way, in whatever order, I recommend that you read all of the sections because you should familiarize yourself as much as possible with the *method* of dealing with your teen-ager's problems, even if a particular problem is not one that you have.

Don't expect instant success. Remember, understanding is a key factor in getting at the heart of solutions to your problems with your teen-ager. Understanding takes time and effort. And it takes some courage on your part to admit that some of your own attitudes toward your teen-ager may be the largest contributing factor to the problems you are having with him or her. To change those attitudes and to begin to work out a synthesis in the family takes patience and a willingness to make mistakes. Don't be afraid to make a mistake. You have made mistakes before. I'm asking you to risk a change in your approach to your teen-age kid to see if you can't turn around a situation that up to now has seemed to be growing increasingly out of control.

Both the questions that you have had about your teen-age kid and the answers are contained in the following pages of this book. If you will study them carefully and bring to them understanding and a willingness to examine some of your own attitudes about your teen-age kid, you will find yourself beginning to treat your kid differently. Your kid also will begin to act differently toward you. It's never too late. Kids don't like tension and problems around the house any more than you do. If you will let them, they will be grateful to you for it, and, in time, maybe even love you for it. Get right to it. You can do it, if you try!

Problem #1

██

"My Kid Won't Take on Responsibility"

Picture yourself arriving home in the evening after a hard day. As you turn your car into the driveway you suddenly have to swerve sharply to avoid running over the new $150 bike you just bought for your teen-ager. At the edge of the drive-way, near where the bike has been abandoned, there are ugly bicycle tire gouges where only just this morning a lovely bed of tulips was growing. As your eyes move to the front porch of the house you catch sight of several bags of garbage deposited care-lessly, the contents spilling out over the steps. Al-most in the same moment you notice that a window in the cellar has been shattered by what looks like the impact of an air rifle pellet.

Appalled, you enter the house and immediately

trip over a pile of books in the front hall. As you rush into the kitchen to find the teen-age child who you know is responsible for all this mess and destruction, you notice that the dirty dishes from an afternoon snack are still sitting on the kitchen table, alongside a report from the School Guidance Counselor complaining that homework is not being done. From upstairs comes the ear-splitting blast of rock music.

You race up the stairs to confront your adolescent, and as you fling open the door the smell of dirty sneakers almost blows you back into the hall. And there, wearing a pair of tattered jeans and a T-shirt with a death's head imprinted across the chest, astride a pile of dirty laundry, scattered sports equipment, soda cans, extension wires, wet towels, candy bar wrappers and gym clothes is your very own teen-ager, looking at you with a big innocent grin from ear to ear.

"Hi, Dad! How was your day?"

Does the scenario seem at all familiar? The complaint of parents who cannot get their teen-agers to act responsibly around the house is a common one, a situation, moreover, that is the cause of much unhappiness on the part of both teen-agers and parents alike.

Of course, it is not just the messiness and carelessness that teen-agers are so prone to that is the main concern to parents; nor is it the fact that time and time again the teen-ager ignores his or her own promise to "shape up." Messiness, carelessness and broken promises are part of the problem, but of far greater importance is the fact that these irresponsible behavior patterns are simply signs to the parents of a deeper underlying lack of responsibility which can only result in the teen-ager growing up and developing into a bum.

What kind of an adult will emerge from a teen-ager who is messy, is indifferent to parental requests, won't take pride in his or her appearance, doesn't do homework, doesn't write thank-you notes to grandparents, and fails to perform assigned chores around the house? Such a person will never get into college, will never be able to hold a decent job, will never amount to anything in the world.

Parents who are concerned about the irresponsibility of their teen-age children are *really* concerned about what this irresponsible behavior means in terms of what is ahead in the future. For many parents, a mess on the outside reflects a messy psyche on the inside. Parents essentially are afraid that their kid will never grow up, that their kid will be unprepared to face life's responsibilities.

Interestingly, I have found that the closer a teen-age boy or girl is to their senior year of high school, the more intensely concerned the parents become over issues of responsibility. The reason is obvious: In our society, a teen-ager who has reached 15, 16 or 17 years is customarily expected to be well on the way toward preparing for greater independence from the parents. In most middle-class, upwardly mobile families this means that the adolescent is expected to enter college and expand his or her intellectual frontiers, improve social relatedness, and with a little luck and guidance identify an area of interest which bears some resemblance, at least, to future career and work interests.

Furthermore, for those teen-agers who do not have

the means, the inclination, or ability to pursue a course of higher education, the latter years of high school are every bit as much, and maybe more so, an important transitional phase toward adult responsibilities. For these students, getting a job is of paramount importance, especially when their parents are unable to continue to provide financial support.

Thus, the matter of the parents' concerns about teen-ager irresponsibility is deeply rooted in the normal expectations of society itself. Feelings, and, indeed, passions, run strong. What so often happens, in my experience, is that the deep-rooted concerns and consequent reactive behavior of the parents contribute to making the problem worse than it is.

The Adolescent View

Adolescence is a time when a child's needs, attitudes and interests are changing rapidly and dramatically. The whirl of activity around a teenager is not just what you see on the outside; it exists, as well, on the inside where even the teenager has to wonder what is going on within. As a result, there just simply isn't much interest in thinking about one's "responsibilities"—at least, not about those things that parents see as responsibilities. The truth is, the teen-ager who once took on the responsibility of emptying the garbage every day like a good little kid suddenly now sees *new and different* responsibilities confronting him that are much more important. For girls, there is *that* boy who has been smiling every day from behind his chemistry book; for boys, there is *that* girl who always seems to swing her hips a little more exaggeratedly when she passes in a corridor; there is a *concert* to go to, another *party* to get ready for. To the teen-ager these are all *new responsibilities* that are much more important than the mere appearance of one's room.

A teen-ager's irresponsible "forgetful" behavior is what is left after the other more urgent responsibilities of the day are taken care of. The teen-ager quite suddenly has entered a new world that is vibrant, often exciting, usually confusing, and sometimes terrifying. For the moment, at least, parents with their expectations for neatness and high performance have become irrelevant. To the teen-ager, their parents' considerations of responsibility are often manifestations of a cosmetic approach to life that is "phony."

With regard to the "future," teen-agers are as concerned about it as the parents. They really are. It's just that they perceive of the future *differently*. To the teen-age girl, the future may be next Saturday night, when for the first time in her life she will face the question of whether or not to kiss the new boy who has asked her out. That's a big decision. Every experience to the teen-ager is somewhat *new*, and requires planning, deep thought. The future is very real to the teen-ager, but time has become compressed. The future is next week, tomorrow, 10 minutes from now. That *other* future of the parents is about as remote as the idea of intelligent life existing on other planets.

There are other aspects to teen-age irresponsibility as well. Although responsible behavior is associated with adulthood, to the teen-ager his behaving responsibly is often perceived as acting like Mommy or Daddy's "good child"—the *very opposite* of being an adult. To act responsibly is to continue to behave like a good little kid. Good children are obedient, polite, answer the phone courteously, are achievers. Around the house they are seen, but not heard. No wonder that the teen-ager on his wild ride into adulthood suddenly has turned into a raucous, inconsiderate, nasty, selfish, foul-mouthed, non-achieving "bad" kid.

In families where children prior to their teen-age years have been given *carte blanche*, with no responsibilities—in other words, where the children, colloquially speaking, have been spoiled—to expect responsible behavior all of a sudden, now that the child is a teen-ager, is to expect a great deal. In such families the transition from childhood to responsible adulthood through the teen-age passage may be more difficult than for other children.

Nevertheless, though it may be hard to believe, moderate teen-age irresponsible behavior is, in many respects, a healthy sign. Oftentimes the child who is considered "good" is a child who is the mirror image of the parents. Psychological evidence points to the fact that sooner or later even "good" children will be obliged to rebel against their parents in order to develop their own adult personalities. Sometimes remaining "good" can cause serious problems for an individual at a later stage in life. In a broad sense, moderate irresponsible behavior on the part of a formerly "good" child is a manifestation of healthy teen-age insurrection. It is a sign that your teen-ager is less concerned about Mommy and Daddy's approval for every "good" deed, and is more interested now in pursuing his or her own path of self-discovery. This is as it should be.

Dealing with Teen-age Irresponsibility

Despite the fact that moderate teen-age irresponsibility is a normal behavior pattern, parents of teen-agers do have their own responsibility to offer some guidance and provide some direction in the case of blatant manifestations of teen-age irresponsible behavior. There is, after all, high school graduation to think about, college, a job, marriage, children, etc., etc. We do not want our children flunking out of school, or driving cars while under the influence of alcohol or drugs, or ending up with an unwanted pregnancy.

So, what to do with the teen-ager who is more irresponsible perhaps than is good for him, than he ought to be?

What I have found in my experience is that the teen-ager who is acting irresponsibly too much of the time is a teen-ager whom the parents are *not permitting* to be responsible. In such instances, there is a tendency to *over-protect* the teen-ager, to treat him as if he still were a child. He is not, in short, held responsible for his own behavior.

Take an example. If a teen-ager keeps forgetting to carry out the garbage, and you keep *reminding* him that he has forgotten to carry out the garbage, he knows that he will never have to think about the garbage again, because his parents will always think about it for him. If, on the other hand, for example, you were to allow the garbage to accumulate so that the refrigerator door is blocked by garbage bags, thus making it impossible for the teen-ager to get his customary afternoon snack, even the most irresponsible teen-ager, in most cases, will eventually take action.

The lesson to the teen-ager here is that if he does not take responsibility for removing the garbage, the garbage will not be removed. Waiting for this lesson to sink in may involve some stoicism, including a strong nose, on the part of the parents. But it is the kind of lesson that very often strikes home.

My feeling is that dealing with irresponsible behavior in teen-agers requires the finest sensitivity on the part of the parents. The important first step is to permit the teen-ager to be responsible for himself, to *step back* and, in a sense, allow the youngster to *reap the consequences* of his own behavior. At the same time, the parent has the added task of giving subtle direction and structure to a teen-ager. Does this sound like a contradiction? It is not, really. What is called for here is some "fine tuning" that can demand on the part of parents the patience of Job and the wisdom of Solomon. Although, without question, you will be available always to give guidance and support to your teen-age child should it be necessary, the ultimate goal should be to put the responsibility that you have assumed for your child all during his formative years squarely, at last, onto the teen-ager himself.

How to Go About It

Before we proceed to the specifics of how to cope with teen-age irresponsibility, let us look at a case study that illustrates clearly, I think, the "fine tuning" required in turning responsibility from the parents over to a teen-ager, while at the same time providing a necessary supporting structure and guidance.

CASE STUDY—RICHARD F.

The Complaint

My first meeting with Richard F. took place in my office with his parents. Encountering this handsome 13-year-old with a voice that was still in the process of alternating between a high squeak and a low baritone, it was hard for me to believe that he was the same person his mother had described over the phone.

Richard was depicted as failing in school, neglecting his homework, ignoring household chores, and acting disagreeably toward both of his parents. The matter that was of utmost urgency to Mr. and Mrs. F. was Richard's reluctance to do his homework and the desultory manner in which he practiced his music lessons on the flute and piano. (At his own request, Richard was learning to play both instruments.)

As far as his homework was concerned, Richard claimed that it was too hard. When his father tried to help him, the boy would often experienced frustration and launched into a temper tantrum, complaining that he couldn't do the work. With regard to his music lessons, Richard oftentimes wouldn't practice at all until the day of his lesson. Because in his mother's opinion he usually wasn't prepared, she would attempt to "get him ready" by going over the lesson with him, at which point Richard would respond by screaming at his mother for interfering, and the practice session would deteriorate into a shouting match.

Another area of conflict in the house was over the matter of clean laundry. Since Richard's mother worked during the day, oftentimes she didn't have time to run a laundry for her son. When he couldn't find clean clothes, which to be truthful, was fairly often, Richard would fly into a rage.

Background

Richard was the only son of Mr. and Mrs. F., though there were two older identical twin sisters, both of whom had graduated from high school and were now attending separate colleges away from home. Mrs. F. was a licensed teacher, and Mr. F. was a successful civil engineer, a *summa cum laude* graduate of Yale.

Richard, it turned out, never had done well in school, and as a result, at a certain point, it was determined through testing that he had a "mild learning disability," the result of poor auditory attention. He could hear perfectly, and he was of average intelligence, but something seemed to prevent him from retaining information that was presented to him orally. He would hear the words, and could repeat them back, even giving an intelligent interpretation of their meaning. But then,

10 minutes later, he would forget much of what had been told to him. Of course, if he was supposed to go bicycle riding with a friend he wouldn't forget. He would only forget those kinds of abstract matters that didn't seem very important to him in terms of his immediate pleasure. This kind of learning disability pattern, incidentally, is not uncommon.

During his early school years, Richard had received private tutoring in selected academic areas, whereas now he was getting "special help" from his *summa cum laude* father.

Aside from battles over Richard's lessons and other manifestations of his "irresponsibility," it was obvious to me that there was genuine warmth and affection on both sides between the parents and their son. Richard was comfortable with his father, and looked forward to "fooling around" with his Dad when homework didn't intrude. He also had an open and joking relationship with his mother, even though the joking often was at Richard's expense, usually around the matter of his "forgetfulness."

Reaching Understanding

During the course of 10 therapy sessions with Richard and his mother and father, it became apparent that Richard's poor academic record was of the utmost concern to the parents. It also became apparent that their concern was manifested in somewhat different ways. Mr. F., considering his son "handicapped," tended to take a warm, nurturing approach to Richard's homework difficulties. Unfortunately, while starting out with the best of intentions, Mr. F. would often lose patience and become angry when Richard's attention would drift off into daydreaming, as it frequently did.

Mrs. F., on the other hand, tended to believe "deep down" that Richard's problems with responsibility had to do partly, at least with his being "spoiled." Her approach was to take a much firmer supervisory attitude toward her son. She would hover over him while he practiced his music lessons, demanding perfection.

Richard would react toward both of his parents similarly. With his father he would throw down a spelling list, for example, insisting that it was "too hard," and that he couldn't do it. In the case of his mother, he would fly into a rage, claiming that she was "interfering" and should "bug off."

As time went on, I came to the idea that what both parents were doing, in different ways, was the same thing. With her own high standards of achievement, Mrs. F. really was interfering with his music practice (just as Richard complained). Not being able to measure up to her demands for perfection tended to reinforce Richard's feelings of low self-esteem, causing him to not want to practice at all. Mr. F., continuing to treat his son as a "handicapped" person, also was unconsciously reinforcing Richard's low estimation of himself. It was easier for Richard to believe he couldn't do his homework than to get down to work and try to do it, especially when Dad was always there to do it for him.

Although it was true that these parents approached their son's problems in diametrically opposite ways—one demanding, the other supporting—the effect in the end was the same. They both did not allow Richard to take responsibility for himself.

Creative Synthesis

When I pointed out to the family what I saw taking place, there was amazement. Mr. F. at first was reluctant to admit that he had been over-compensating for his son's perceived deficiencies, but finally, after thinking about it, admitted that not only was it true, but that he had been doing it partly to counteract his wife's more demanding approach. Mrs. F., on the other hand, when she was able to acknowledge that her interference with Richard's music practice was perhaps the result of her own high expectations, added that her behavior probably had been exaggerated by her secret feelings that her husband was "spoiling" Richard.

Once this was out in the open, there seemed to be a general sigh of relief by everyone. Everybody recognized, at least, what had been going on. Mr. and Mrs. F. immediately agreed to make some important changes. Mr. F. promised to leave all aspects of Richard's music lessons to his music teacher. If his music teacher flunked him out of class, they all agreed, it would be *Richard's responsibility*, not his mother's. (Since Richard loved music and was quite talented, it was immediately obvious to me that he would never allow himself to flunk his music.) For his part, Mr. F. agreed to "help" Richard with his homework, but only after his son had studied first on his own. It was at this point that Mr. F. recalled that the school guidance counselor for some time had been stating that Richard showed every sign of being able to do his schoolwork on his own, and that he should therefore, be responsible for his own academic progress—his failures as well as successes.

Richard, of course, greeted these proposed changes

on the part of his parents with enthusiasm. But because he *really had* been spoiled, to some extent, by the over-concern of his parents for many years, it was not at all certain in anybody's mind, including my own, that Richard would do his part, particularly with regard to his school work. It was then that the "fine tuning" and sensitivity of the parents came into play. Good intentions were one thing, but "following through" was another. A little structure was introduced into the deal that was made. Mr. and Mrs. F. said that in return for their granting Richard sole responsibility for doing his homework and practicing his music, he would have to set aside certain specific times for these activities, and then hold to the schedule. A pact was made that until his homework and practicing were done, he would not ask to go out with his friends.

Shortly after the new "ground rules" were established and accepted by all members of the family, several positive changes occurred. Without the demanding presence of his mother, Richard felt confident enough about his music to join the school band, and within a very short time was accepted as a "bandsman" member. With this step toward progress, Richard's parents quickly dropped the rule about setting aside a strict time to practice his music. He was now "grown up enough," they told him, to decide on his own when he wanted to practice, a clear sign to Richard that they were accepting him as an adult, something they had never been able to do before!

Richard still didn't find it easy to do his homework, but he was firmly encouraged to attempt it on his own, and when he showed the slightest signs of progress, he was praised in the strongest terms.

When he would get "stuck," his father would volunteer to help him. This consistent approach seemed to lower the anger and impatience level on both sides, and there was a noticeable improvement in Richard's homework.

With the recognition now dawning on everyone in the family that, despite his validated early learning disability, Richard was developing into a "normal" young man who could manage to work around his auditory learning problems if he tried, it also began to become clear that there were certain other "normal responsibilities" having to do with taking care of himself that Richard had been "protected from" for many years. With this thought in mind, Mr. F. suggested to Richard that if clean clothes were not always available at the instant he wanted them, there was a very good reason for it—and also a very easy way to remedy the situation. He could learn to operate the washing machine and do the laundry himself.

The end result of this very successful case was that two months after our last session Mr. F. called to tell me that all grades had moved upward on Richard's report card and that Richard had learned how to operate the washing machine by himself!

Practical Steps

In the case of Richard F. we have seen an almost classic example of a teen-ager who wanted and needed to take on responsibility for himself, but for a variety of reasons was refusing to do so. What was required here, as is so often true in the case of irresponsible teenagers, was for the *parents*, first, to realize that it was *they* who were standing in the way of Richard's taking on responsibility. By backing off a bit, they put the responsibility where it belonged—on Richard's shoulders. At the same time, they did not just "throw him to the sharks." They negotiated a *structure* around which Richard could plan his activities, thus providing a support while leaving him in charge of himself. In this case there are some fundamental lessons about helping your child to become more responsible.

I. Don't panic. Don't punish

An "increase" in irresponsible behavior on the part of teen-agers very often is *not* an increase in irresponsibility at all. Much of the time it is just a heightened perception by the parents that their teen-ager is on the threshold of becoming a young adult; the parents begin to demand things from their children that they never demanded before. "You're getting to the age now when you should begin to," etc., is the usual refrain.

And this heightened concern by the parents comes at the very time when the teen-ager is trying to find his own identity and tends to equate the demands of his parents that he be more responsible with being "treated like a little kid." Thus, there is a clash of perceived interests. Every family with teenage children has the same experience. Some kids are more responsible than others, but the basic pattern is the same for all.

The tendency of the parents is to exaggerate the importance and degree of their children's irresponsibility. Many parents mistakenly believe their teen-ager is purposefully trying to hurt their feelings by behaving irresponsibly. If you panic and

start "getting on your kid's case" over every irresponsible act, you will not only drive your kid crazy;
you will drive yourself crazy, as well. Certainly
punishment—"teaching the kid a lesson," withholding something from your child that he wants,
"grounding"—these punishment approaches are
particularly inappropriate when the issue is getting
your teen-ager to act responsibly. Punishment in
this case tends only to harden both sides into the
opposing roles they have taken on.

II. Let your kid be responsible for himself

As we saw in the case of Richard F., while his
parents were complaining that he wasn't responsible, at the same time they weren't permitting him
to take on responsibility for himself. In their efforts
to "help" him, they were actually hindering him
from growing up.

True, there were long-standing valid reasons for
his parents taking charge of Richard's academic
progress. But as Richard turned into his teen-age
years, he began to change from needing so much
help. His parents simply missed seeing that the
change was taking place.

A "helpful" parent who constantly reminds a son
to do his homework or who takes on the responsibility of awakening a late sleeping daughter is only
maintaining the existing state of affairs. The son
will always rely on someone else to be responsible
for his homework, and the daughter will rely on her
parents to be her alarm clock. Only after Richard's
mother left all aspects of his music instruction to
the music teacher and after his father relinquished
the lion's share of the responsibility for his school-

work did he begin to behave in a more responsible manner and make progress in both areas.

I cannot emphasize it too strongly: Place responsibility where it belongs—on the teen-ager. And don't be afraid if it doesn't work out perfectly at first. Parents tend to want to be perfect, and to want their kids to be perfect. *Nobody* is perfect, in case you need to be told. Your kid may actually have to *fail* a few times before he begins to get the message that the responsibility for not failing is his own. You may actually have to experience the "humiliation" of knowing that your kid is in the lowest five percent of the class. So be it. Despite his *braggadocio* efforts to separate himself from you, your teen-ager is probably more like you than either he or you believe. Before he finishes, in order to escape the same feelings of humiliation that you are experiencing, he will almost certainly begin to try harder.* If *you* care (and you do, or you wouldn't be reading this book), you can almost be certain that sooner or later your kid will care, too. This is a *very important point*, in my opinion. Keep it strongly in mind and let it serve to relax you and reassure you if you think at the moment that your kid is more irresponsible than he should be.

III. Encourage your teen-ager

Allowing your child to take responsibility for himself does not mean abandoning him. The sensitivity, or "fine tuning," that I have referred to should come into play. Start off by stepping back and letting your teen-ager take responsibility for

---

*Obviously, a child who persistently performs unsatisfactorily in school should be tested for eyesight, dyslexia, general health and nutrition, and/or other factors that might be contributing to a learning disability.

himself. Observe what is going on. Most likely you will be surprised to see some areas where your teenager willingly takes on some responsibility; maybe there will be other areas where he "goofs off." Try to encourage your child in the strong areas. In the case of Richard, his music was an obvious area to work with. Although his mother no longer interfered with his practicing, when he took the first step and indicated that he wanted a new flute for Christmas, she saw to it that he got it, and got a good one. When he expressed interest in a particular recording, Mr. F. made sure that he got the tape, too.

Toward the very end of our therapy sessions Richard announced during the session that he thought he might like to go to music school someday. I hope you can appreciate how thrilled we all were to hear him say it. His statement went way beyond his interest in music alone; it implied, for the first time, an interest in his *own future*; it implied that he might want to go to college; a further implication was that he would take on the responsibility of improving his other grades, along with his continued progress in music, in order to qualify himself for college. These matters were all casually and gently discussed, *having grown naturally out of Richard's own interest*. Mr. and Mrs. F. encouraged Richard further by mentioning several colleges where the curriculum was strong in music. All of this, I believe, played a role in furthering Richard's sense of responsibility.

IV. The matter of structure

As we saw in the case of Richard, there is nothing wrong with introducing a little structure into your teen-ager's life. It lets your teen-ager know that even though you are willing to step back and "let him alone," there are some *obligations* that have to be met. A bit of old-fashioned horse-trading is indicated here.

"Yes, I will no longer interfere in the performance of your homework. At the same time, I do expect you to set aside a certain time to do that homework, and to stick to the schedule." This is the contract that was made with Richard by his parents. Perhaps you will have to find a different formula. The same formula does not work for every child.

"I know that you need time to be with your friends after school. If you'll set aside a certain time to do your homework, and stick to it, I'll let you off from emptying the garbage for the rest of the school term." What a concession that would be! But it might work. Or, "I'm not going to bother you ever again about your homework. If you bring up that 'D' in Algebra to a 'C', you deserve to get the new BMX bike you want so badly."

Don't be afraid to *let up* on some responsibilities that previously have been imposed. Pick those areas that are of most concern, and work on those, and in return for progress made, think about letting up on some other demands that you have been making. Sometimes a teen-ager will act irresponsibly because he feels he is being given *too many* responsibilities in too many areas.

Finally, remember that we are talking here about *teen-agers*, not adults. Do not expect your teen-ager—not ever, as long as he is a teen-ager—to be as responsible as you are. If your teen-ager was as responsible as you are, he wouldn't be a teen-ager.

Expect your kid to forget once in awhile to turn out the lights when he goes to bed.

Expect your kid occasionally to forget to turn off the TV.

Expect your kid now and then to leave a mess around the sink when she finishes experimenting with her make-up.

Expect every so often to find books and clothes dumped on the living room floor after school.

I'm not saying that you shouldn't admonish your teen-age kids when they do these things. After all, that's *your* responsibility: namely, to guide your teen-ager into becoming a civilized adult. But what I am saying is that these trivial acts of irresponsibility are the hallmarks of teen-age behavior, and, in my experience, though they are sometimes frustrating and annoying, do not in and of themselves mean all that much. One fine day you will come upon your teen-ager picking up his or her own room without having been asked to do it. Yes, it actually happens. One day your son will be bored, and for some unknown reason—perhaps he wants to make a few dollars—he will mow the lawn when it needs it. I wouldn't suggest that you hold your breath until the time comes, but as your teen-ager becomes older, he or she will notice things that need to be done around the house, and will even begin to help out by doing some of them. (They may complain to you first that *you* haven't done them.) You should encourage and reward every little sign of growth.

In the meantime, remember that you are still dealing with *children*. Enjoy their child-like qualities as much as you can. At least *be tolerant*. Do not overburden them with so many responsibilities that they cannot be children. They will be leaving your home one of these days—sooner than you think. Believe it or not, you will miss them very much. Enjoy them while you have them—with their faults, as well as their virtues. That's part of being a parent, too.

Problem #2

~~~~~~

"Why Is My Kid So Full of Anger?"

When your child was still a toddler, adored by Grandpa and Grandma, an outburst of anger was an accepted form of behavior.

"Oh, he's just having a temper tantrum," Grandpa would say. And you either picked your child up and hugged him, or left him alone to cry his heart out, or tried to divert his attention to other things, or maybe even gave him a sharp scolding or other form of punishment.

Remember the "terrible two"? Your child was a "terror" back then. The reason for it was that you were locked in a struggle with him over various issues of who was going to be the "boss." A perfect example is the issue of toilet training. You wanted your child to "let go" at a certain time into the potty. Your child was still fighting for the right to "let go" when and where he wanted to, usually in his pants. In some cases, the child learned easily that he must move his bowels into a toilet, rather than into his pants; in other cases, there may have been a period of struggle before the matter was concluded.

The important thing is that sooner or later the child became toilet trained. In short, you directed the child's behavior into civilized channels.

Now, all of a sudden, your child is a teen-ager, and you are locked again in a struggle for control. The teen-ager is struggling for control over his own destiny; you are struggling to maintain the control that you feel he is too young to do without. This time the battle is not so one-sided, because your child has ideas and thoughts of his own, and the wherewithal to fight back.

Although your child is a tougher adversary now, he still may not have the experience necessary to win his battle for control of his life by logical argument. Even when logic is all on his side, and even if he knows all the arguments, you still may not be willing to relinquish your control over him. And, let's face it, you've still got the *power*. So the teenage youngster oftentimes has no recourse but to become resentful, and react with anger.

I Really Don't Like My Own Kid Anymore

Anger, from any source, is threatening. But anger coming from one's own flesh and blood can be one of the most unsettling experiences you can

have. At first, you can't believe it is happening.
There is a sense of shock and amazement at the
intensity of the assault. Before long your shock
turns into concern. And soon the concern may turn
into actual fear. Not necessarily fear of physical
violence—though in some cases that fear can exist—but more often as a general anxiety that takes
the form of you feeling like a failure: That you
have done "something wrong"; that there must be
a worm in the core of the family's existence. You
thought you knew how to deal with your kid, and
now it turns out that all those years of loving attention and training have been to no avail. Suddenly you find that you are getting angry, too. You
may actually reach a point of concluding that you
really *don't like* your child anymore. This, by the
way, only contributes further to your feelings of
failure.

Well, don't despair. These feelings are all natural! We all have felt them from time to time, if not
toward our children, certainly toward other loved
ones—toward our own parents, for instance. What
little child hasn't at one time or another, cried out,
"I hate you, Mommy!" But we lived through it; so
did our parents. And now that you are the parent
you will live through it too.

Serious Business

I don't mean to minimize your feelings of fear,
frustration, anger and failure; nor do I mean to minimize or dismiss altogether the importance of intense displays of teen-age anger. Nevertheless, it
should be reassuring to you to know that in my ex-

perience often the most extreme instances of repeated anger outbursts were the easiest and quickest to resolve.

We know that the teen-ager is struggling during these development years to determine and control his own destiny. Following 12 years, more or less, of having been provided with the guidelines of life, the teen-ager is now compelled, by nature, to declare his own independence. He wants the world to know that he is no longer willing simply to acquiesce in the parents' imperatives.

Okay, you say, but why does the anger have to be so forceful? To answer that question, consider for a moment the situation of the teen-ager. All his life Mom and Dad have been responsible for his well-being, his very existence. All decisions, all responsibility, have rested with Mom and Dad. Upkeep of the house, mortgage and/or rent payments, decisions as to what kind of car to buy, where to go for a family vacation—all were matters decided hitherto by Mom and Dad.

Suddenly the teen-ager realizes that he is *different* from his parents. The frustrating part is that he has no wherewithal to launch out on his own. He is still dependent upon Mom and Dad for life's necessities, not to mention life's amenities, until he becomes a full adult. This fact of nature, in itself, can cause feelings of resentment. How can the teen-ager *demonstrate* that he is different, that he is yearning for independence? One obvious way is through his irascibility.

Moreover, because the teen-ager is determined to strike out on his own, he is in the process of *rejecting the support*, the "security blanket," provided by his parents. This is a terrifying time for many teen-agers because they are testing themselves for the first time, and they do not always feel adequate to the task they insist on setting for themselves. Teenagers who are not coping well in the world they are testing frequently become frightened. A fearful creature may be likely to retaliate against restraints, or authority, or even efforts to be helpful, in resentful and angry ways.

The inadequacy that the teen-ager feels in the real world is often seen as stemming from an inadequacy in the parents. For example, anger can exist because the parents don't have as much money as other kids' parents; or the parents are divorced, with the parent who has moved out (most often the father, but not always) resented; or the other partner is resented for having driven his or her mate out; or rules established by one parent are not consistent with demands made by the other parent.

What to Do?

Anger in the house is unpleasant. At the same time, for reasons indicated, a certain amount of teen-age anger is inevitable. What can you as a parent do to initiate a change in the family relationships that will ease the angry tension and result in a synthesis of common attitudes that will be acceptable to the whole family?

Before we examine some possible ways to approach your teenager's angry outbursts, let's take a look at two case studies from my own experience of working with two angry teen-agers—one, a boy,

Michael T., 15; the other, a girl, Rebecca N., 14.

CASE STUDY I—MICHAEL T.

The Complaint

Michael T. came to me as a result of a frantic phone call one night from his mother who stated that her son was on the verge of "killing" her, that he was threatening to run away from home, and that he was destroying furniture in the house.

When I saw Michael at the first of two family sessions, he did not appear to me to be the "wild beast" that his parents claimed he was becoming. He seemed very much in control of his emotions (more so than his parents, as a matter of fact), though he admitted to feelings of rage toward both of his parents, with particular fury for his mother who he said was "over-protective."

Although he was passing all his courses in school, he recently for the first time in his life had cut a few classes, and on one occasion had refused to go to school. At the first therapy session he said that on the night his mother had called me he had run out of the house after pushing over a lamp, because he had been afraid of striking her.

At this same first session, Mr. and Mrs. T. were in agreement that Michael was untrustworthy, abusive, and no longer cared about anyone in the home except himself.

Background

The T. family recently had moved from a neighboring town to their current location. At first Michael had experienced considerable difficulty in adjusting. Whereas he had been accepted by his peers in the previous town, he was now somewhat on the defensive with his peers for appearing meek and a "momma's boy."

The label "momma's boy" was put on Michael primarily because he had been brought up to be very respectful and polite to adults, in conformity with the upbringing of the parents. Michael's family was originally from Spain and he had been raised within a culture whose demands and expectations were quite different from the subculture of the town where they currently resided. In accordance with the cultural values of their country of origin, children were the sole responsibility of the mother. *Teen-agers were still considered children* until they either worked or moved away from home. Such new customs as staying out late at night went against the code of good child-rearing, and Mr. and Mrs. T. were entrenched in this set attitude.

Michael, on the other hand, was determined to measure up to his peers. He was making a point of submerging his "soft" side. He was trying to develop a "thick skin" to stay on top and for emotional survival. He suddenly was as adamant about developing his own lifestyle as his parents were about maintaining the standards of their own cultural values. Hence, the two sides were at complete odds.

Reaching Understanding

Michael's rebellion against his parents, and the concomitant anger at their stubbornness, was in his case an *act of survival*, as well as of self-discovery. He was trying to obliterate any vestige of behavior that linked him to his mother's approach to child-rearing and her demand for docility.

It was apparent to me from the start that Michael really was a very nice young man who was struggling desperately to find his own identity in the face of fixed parental ideas that ran counter to his own. This opinion that he was a nice young man was reinforced by comments of the school's guidance counselor who stated that Michael was well liked by teachers and students alike, even though he had experienced some difficulty in recent weeks.

During our brief course of therapy Michael confessed that he felt that most of his problems were related to a new circle of friends he was trying to cultivate at school. This was a group that thought it was "cool" to cut classes and "hang out" at the local gas station and refreshment stand. Michael saw the new group as outgoing, carefree, and very much the opposite of his "uptight" parents. He was choosing this group, in fact, precisely to escape the inhibitions of the parental environment.

At the same time, despite his attraction to the new group, Michael admitted in the presence of his parents at only the second of our sessions that he was beginning to feel that his circle was becoming a bad influence on him. He saw a direct connection between "hanging out" with the gang and cutting classes, and it worried him.

Creative Synthesis

Michael's admission was the key to his parents' being able to begin to understand their son better. They had begun to lose sight of the fact that Michael was capable of good judgment on his own, that he was capable after a few experimentations to question his own behavior. Once the parents regained their perspective on Michael, they were able to relax a bit. They were no longer so worried about losing a son, nor fearful that their love for him would disappear because of his contemptible behavior and anger toward them.

This change in their own attitude, in turn, led to an immediate reduction in Michael's level of tension and anger. The new understanding suddenly cleared the way for a creative synthesis of the various points of view existing within this essentially loving family. When Michael's parents explained in a much calmer atmosphere how highly they regarded the need for a structured home life, Michael was able to tell them that *he also* believed in curfews, and on the importance of education, and in the establishment of rules. What he wanted, he said, was *more reasonableness* in the establishment of the rules.

Almost immediately Mr. and Mrs. T. tried expressing their expectations for responsible behavior in a new and less threatening way. New "more reasonable" curfew hours were established. New ways of expressing parental restraints were worked out. (For example, instead of threatening, the family would now say: "Please tell us where *you have decided* you are going to go tonight, and please be home by midnight.")

Within four weeks of our first meeting, Mrs. T. called to cancel our next session. "Michael is his same old sweet self," she chirrupped. And I believed her.

CASE STUDY II—REBECCA N.

The Complaint

Rebecca N. was 14 years old when she was referred to me for therapy in connection with her violent temper, general disagreeableness and unhappy demeanor. Rebecca had a habit of telling anyone who would listen that her family was "horrible," and that she hated them all. She was critical of her older sister, Sally, 16, and of her next younger sibling, Penny, 12.

Rebecca harbored her harshest criticism for her mother who didn't behave "as a mother should," in her opinion. Mrs. N., a divorcee, and very attractive, had a variety of boyfriends. When she would bring any one of her male friends home for the girls to meet, Rebecca would be as obnoxious and unpleasant as possible.

In response to Rebecca's anger, the other sisters and her mother retaliated angrily on their own, thus setting off a new cycle of angry behavior on the part of Rebecca. This is a common phenomenon sometimes referred to by psychologists as "a feedback loop." The cycle of retaliation seems to loop back on itself, rising in intensity. This was what was happening in Rebecca's family, so that there was practically no communication, and even well-intentioned efforts to help Rebecca resulted only in creating more anger.

The Background

Rebecca's mother was not merely divorced, but the father had "walked out" of their home four years earlier, leaving Mrs. N. with four daughters to raise.

All four daughters, including Rebecca, excelled in their grades at school. However, Rebecca's older sister, Sally, was extremely popular among her classmates, going around with the "in" clique. Like her mother, she dated a lot of different boys, a pattern that horrified Rebecca. The idea of being kissed on the lips was particularly repulsive to her.

Rebecca's next younger sibling, Penny, was also popular and had achieved special distinction as a broad jumper on the school track team.

Rebecca never seemed happy, complaining about her looks (even though she was pretty). She considered herself "different" from other boys and girls her own age. It was common among members of the family to compare her with her absent father who was said by the mother to have a "terrible disposition just like you."

In the course of meeting with both the mother and daughter, it became obvious that Rebecca felt bitter at her father for having "abandoned" her. Moreover, the complaint was legitimate, since the father rarely visited the children. But Rebecca's feeling of abandonment carried over to her mother, too, who Rebecca felt cared more about "all those creepy men" than she did about her daughter.

At a time in her life when she did not know quite

how to fit into the world and needed support, her perception was that there was no one who cared very much about her. she was pretty angry about it.

Reaching Understanding

In therapy sessions with Rebecca and Mrs. N. it soon became apparent that Rebecca was not the only one in the family who was filled with anger. The mother, too, was bitterly resentful at her former husband. Mrs. N. had been left with the job of being a single parent to four daughters, no small task. Her own desirability as a female, moreover, had been brought into question, as well. The reason she valued so highly her popularity with men friends (the "creeps," to Rebecca) was that it offered reassurance that she was still attractive (which she was).

Mrs. N. simply could not understand why Rebecca didn't appreciate her mother's sense of loss and betrayal; or why Rebecca couldn't see how difficult it was for her to bring up four daughters; or why Rebecca had to embarrass her in front of her male friends whom she brought home for the girls to meet.

After several therapy sessions, Mrs. N. began to recognize her own bitter resentments (something she had at first refused to admit). She began to realize also that she and Rebecca were closer in temperament than she had realized. In fact, Mrs. N. and Rebecca were the closest in temperament of all the females in the house.

It was at this point that Mrs. N. began to see Rebecca in a new light. She began to understand the pain and hurt and feelings of abandonment and inadequacy in her daughter. She began to realize that she was expecting *too much maturity* from Rebecca at a time when her daughter was only at the beginning stage of moving forward toward maturity. Once these insights began to sink in, Mrs. N. was then able to modify her retaliative anger and resentment at Rebecca. In fact, she began to realize that what Rebecca needed most was what she herself needed: reassurance and support. Although she herself was able to get this, to some extent, from her social popularity, her daughter was at a point in her life when she did not know yet how to go about doing it.

Creative Synthesis

Without ever mentioning the matter of anger, or the reasons behind the anger, Mrs. N. began simply to take time to help Rebecca build a more positive estimation of herself. Both the mother and I gently called it to Rebecca's attention when she accentuated her negative or undesirable qualities. At the same time, we began to support her positive attributes (such as her adorable smile, a compassionate feeling toward others, her sound moral values).

As she began to wonder if she might not be a worthwhile person after all, Rebecca showed a willingness to attend some of the school social events. And when she remarked on how attractive some of the other girls were, her mother suggested in a nonpushy way that she might want to enroll in a grooming course at the local Y in order to learn the art of applying make-up.

Rebecca picked up on the suggestion, and almost

overnight her appearance improved and, more important, she began to feel a sense of confidence and pleasure with herself.

She was still leary of boys, and balked at suggestions as to how to be more vivacious with them. It was then that her mother, in a stroke of insight, suggested that Rebecca's "quiet confidence" was *even better* than vivaciousness. Rebecca immediately picked up on the phrase "quiet confidence" and began to project that in her relationships with her peers.

After that, the going went comparatively easily. Rebecca actually began to date a boy, something she had never been able to do before. And most importantly, she was having fewer periods of resentment toward her sisters and mother, only rare outbursts of anger, and diminishing brooding moods.

Practical Steps

The two case studies cited are quite different. Yet, in both cases, when the parents were able to understand their children better, and understand where the anger was coming from, they were able to adjust their own behavior in such a way as to *help their teen-ager overcome the underlying problems* that were causing the anger.

As different as each of these case studies appears to be, they nevertheless both bring out some fundamentally sound ways of dealing with teen-age anger.

I. Attitude

The first bit of advice I would give to any parent trying to deal with teen-age anger is *don't panic*. If suddenly you feel you don't know your own child; or if you feel as though you *don't want* to know your child; or even begin to think you *dislike* your own child, accept it for the moment. Both Michael's parents and Rebecca's mother all felt fearful and resentful and angry at the sudden "inexplicable" behavior of their children. *These are natural and understandable initial feelings.*

You're a human being, too. Your teen-ager is provoking the emergence of your basest survival instincts by making unreasonable demands, abusing you, and behaving as if he or she were the only important person in the world whose own ideas ought to be unquestioningly obeyed. No human being likes to be bullied. *It is perfectly understandable to want to retaliate.*

II. The matter of retaliation

Nevertheless, despite your own initial feelings of anger, my strongest advice is: *Don't retaliate!* At least, *try* not to. Don't come up with threats and punishments of your own. You know now that there is an *underlying reason* for your teen-ager's anger. It is partly a natural response on the teen-ager's part to all those years of being controlled. It actually may even "feel good" to the teen-ager to "let go" at *you*, for a change.

Parental retaliation against teen-age anger often only makes the situation worse, because it reinforces the basis of the original anger (as we saw in the cases of both Michael and Rebecca). Particularly, punishment in the form of taking away privileges, etc., does not work to dispel anger. It may dispel, briefly, *manifestations* of anger, but it only builds up resentment.

I have found that in most cases the teen-ager who has been brought up with a sense of society's normative values regarding authority, outward displays of emotion, and empathy for one's fellow man will feel as unhappy about a sudden outburst of anger as you do. He may, in fact, feel outright sorrow and guilt. If there is no terrible retribution inflicted on the teen-ager the first few times that there are incidents of anger outbursts, oftentimes the youngster's own sense of the "rightness of things" will assert itself, and the teen-ager will incorporate self-discipline into his new emerging personality, and hold back from angry outbursts. Understanding is important during this period. The teen-ager *needs time* to make some decisions about himself.

Instead of trying to retaliate, try to determine what the underlying problems are that may be causing the angry outbursts. The more severe the anger, the harder you have to work to seek under-standing of what is going on. In many, many cases it is just a simple matter of your trying to treat your 16-year-old like a six-year-old. It may be time now for you to re-examine some of the rules.

Try to understand better the patterns of the teen-age culture in which your child is living. If the norm of staying out has risen from 11 P.M. to midnight, consider the possibility, at least, of letting your teen-ager stay out until midnight—if not every night, maybe on one night a week. In return for the concession, you can probably exact a promise of prompt return at that hour.

III. Listen carefully

It is always hard to determine precisely how much a teen-ager's anger is "justified," and how much of it is unreasonable. *Listen carefully* to what your teen-ager is blurting out at you. Try to read between the lines of the insults, the complaints, the demands. It will be hard, of course. Your child's anger will often be directed at hurting your feelings, or probing for weakness, or even trying to bully you.

These tactics are all *cries for help*. If you can hold back your anger long enough to try to find out where help is needed, two things will happen: You will begin to be able to deal with your child's problems, and your child will begin to understand that you really are a supportive parent, and not just an obstacle to his or her own progress.

And don't be afraid to let your child know that he is hurting your feelings with his angry outbursts. Don't do it in a way to make your child feel guilty. But when it is an honest statement about your own inner core feelings, frequently a teen-ager will have the sensitivity—and love for you—to let you in and tell you what his underlying problems are, instead of abusing you further with anger.

IV. Re-examine the rules

At a non-angry time try to explain to your teen-ager that although there absolutely *have to be rules in the house*, perhaps some of the old rules should be re-examined. Explain to your teen-ager that you are willing to work out new rules, and sit down together and go about doing just that. Give in as much as you can, while holding the line where you feel it is absolutely essential.

These are some of the approaches you can try in dealing with the anger of your adolescent. The most important things to remember are: Don't retaliate; try to understand what the underlying problems are; deal with your child reasonably, honestly, in a supportive and reassuring way; and at an appropriate calm moment try to work out rules of behavior in the house everyone can accept and feel comfortable with.

Problem #3

//

"My Kid Lies to Me"

Is there anyone anywhere in the world above the age of three who doesn't know the story about the little shepherd boy who cried "Wolf"? As the legend goes, the little fellow twice called out for help, and when the villagers raced to the little boy's rescue, each time it turned out that there was no wolf; the little boy simply had been having a laugh at the villagers' expense. Later, when a real wolf did appear, and the little boy cried "Wolf!" again, the people ignored him, and the wolf ate him up.

So much for little boys who lie or tell tall stories to their mommies and daddies and other grown-ups in town.

The universal familiarity with the story of the little boy who cried "Wolf!" is indicative of the importance our society places on telling the truth. Even more interesting, the punishment of *death* for what could be viewed as not much more than the expression of a child's overactive imagination further underlines the seriousness with which society looks upon lying.

There are good reasons, of course, for instilling the need to tell the truth into humans at an early age. All modern societies depend to a certain extent upon the good faith and trust of the people who live in them. If everyone in society was a liar, then nobody could believe anything or anybody, and the matter of living together in any kind of harmony would break down completely. It is no wonder that "Thou Shalt Not Lie (Bear False Witness)" is one of the Biblical Ten Commandments.

Husbands and wives try to tell each other the truth. When they start lying, usually it's a sign that the marriage is coming apart. Even governments, to one extent or another, are obliged to pay some regard to the truth. Abraham Lincoln wasn't kidding when he said, "You can fool some of the people all of the time, and you can fool all of the people some of the time, but you cannot fool all of the people all of the time." He was right. And when a government is caught in a lie, the wrath of the people is implacable, as witness the unrelenting pursuit of former President Nixon and his staff by the press in connection with the Watergate cover-up.

When very small children "make up" stories, such as that they have an "invisible friend," everyone thinks it's cute—and it is. And, in fact, such stories are a natural and acceptable part of the fantasy life of small children. Even a direct lie implicating the invisible friend in the invasion of a cookie jar is not all that serious, because little children are not adept at lying, and usually they forget to wipe the tell-tale jam off their faces. We tell our small children that they should "always tell Mommy the truth" and if lying incidents don't happen very often, we are satisfied that our message is getting across to them successfully.

When youngsters reach the teen-age years, however, lying takes on a much greater significance. The consequences of lies are greater, because they have to do with such things as automobiles, drugs, liquor, sex, homework, etc.—all matters that are not quite so trivial as invading the cookie jar. As a result, it is very common for parents of teen-agers to become quite panicky over teen-age lying. When a teen-ager lies to parents, the parents very often have a sense suddenly that the greatest of calamities has befallen them.

"I can't trust my own child!" is a parent's cry of despair. Lying by a teen-ager seems to signal to parents that their child is completely out of control. We have seen already (in Problem #2: Anger) that a battle for control is a natural part of the teen-age transition to young adulthood. If parents are unable to determine the truth of a situation—if their child is deliberately and defiantly shutting them out—the world starts to spin crazily. The parents feel there is no way to exercize influence whatsoever, and it can be a terrifying realization. It can provoke anger (fury), depression, feelings of failure, deep anxiety, and even abandonment of trying to deal with the problem at all.

Why Teen-agers Lie

Human beings of all ages tend to want to avoid trouble. There are exceptions to this generality, of course. But, by and large, people prefer to stay out of trouble and to avoid ill feeling. Very often this means avoiding a confrontation. The businessman, for example, who has his secretary tell a caller whom he doesn't want to talk to that he is "in conference" is telling a "white lie" to avoid unpleasantness. A housewife who doesn't want to accept an invitation to a certain dinner party may plead an illness in the family, or make up some other "story" so as to avoid unpleasantness with a person whom she doesn't want to offend directly.

When an adult prevaricates in the manner described it is known as "being tactful." When an adolescent who is out with his friends and doesn't want to bother calling home tells his parents that he couldn't get to a phone, that's a *lie.* True, the teenager who doesn't call home may be causing more anxiety than is the businessman who won't take a call from an insurance salesman. Still, the motive in both cases is very similar. The businessman and the teen-ager are both trying to avoid unpleasantness.

If teen-agers were as sophisticated as adults, they would probably show better judgment about the kinds of lies they tell and when they tell them. But they are not very sophisticated, and they tend to tell lies at inappropriate times and in inappropriate circumstances.

In an attempt to avoid unpleasantness, a teenager often will lie to *postpone the consequence of* some calamity that has already taken place. If Dad doesn't find out until tomorrow that his teen-age daughter has dented the fender on his new Corvette, then tonight she will not have to pay the consequences. That's 12 more hours of avoiding grief! And maybe—just maybe—Dad will never see the dent! Or he'll think he did it himself! Teen-agers are just inexperienced enough and unrealistic enough to sometimes believe that, miraculously, a day of reckoning will not have to come.

There are as many different motives for telling lies as there are people to invent them, but among teen-agers some kinds of lies do fall into a common pattern.

In an effort to *exercise their independence*, teenagers sometimes will tend to be evasive. Evasiveness may not be intended as a deliberate outright lie—certainly it will not be seen as such by the teenager—but it is a way of telling *less than the whole truth*.

"Where are you going tonight?" the parents ask the teen-ager.

And the teen-ager replies, "Oh, just down to the pizza parlor." A more truthful answer might be, "I don't really know what I am going to do, and I'm not sure whether or not you have a right to know, or whether or not I want to tell you. Sometime during the evening I probably will look into the pizza parlor to see if anything is going on, and then I'll make a decision."

The fact is that the teen-ager wants to keep open a variety of options, and furthermore doesn't want to spell them all out to his parents. This is true partly because he feels he has reached an age when he shouldn't have to, and also because just possibly one of the options might be objected to by his parents. So it is not surprising that his answer to the question as to where he is going is evasive.

If, for example, one of the boy's friends with a motorcycle (unregistered for the street) should meet him on the way to the pizza parlor, and the two of them decide to ride to the next town, that's something that Mom and Dad would never permit. So better not tell them. "What they don't know won't hurt them." Or, more to the point, "What they don't know, won't hurt *me*."

The real problem develops after Mom and Dad find out what their son has been doing (as a result of a phone call from the police who have trucked the unregistered bike away to the police station). At that point, the earlier statement by their son that he was going down to "the pizza parlor" is perceived as a deliberate lie. It certainly was less than the whole truth. Frequently parents in such circumstances cannot understand why their teen-ager is not forthcoming with the whole truth. "Why didn't you tell us there was a possibility of going to the next town on your friend's motorcycle?" the parents will ask. "We would have understood." Parents will say this kind of thing after the fact, in an effort to be reasonable and also in a probably futile attempt to keep the same thing from happening again.

"Yeah, sure," the kid mumbles to himself. "No way. They won't even let me ride my *bicycle* to the corner store at night for fear I'll get hit by a truck. Forget it."

Thus, the teen-ager is willing to risk the consequences of being caught riding on the illegal motorcycle rather than spell it all out in advance and be told he can't go out.

This evasive attitude of teen-agers is especially apparent in instances where the youngsters feel that the parents adhere too rigidly to out-of-date standards with regard to such things as curfews and dating rules. The teen-ager knows that the minute he reveals his real plans, he will be blocked. He would rather risk a lie and get caught than tell the truth and have to abide by the "corny," even embarrassing (to him), narrow rules of his parents.

When they go beyond evasiveness, lies sometimes are a cover for teen-agers to save face for a perceived inadequacy within themselves. The teen who tells his parents he is doing "okay" in school when he is failing or who doesn't bring home a report card (forging his parents' signatures), may be attempting to perpetuate a cherished myth held by the parents that their son or daughter is an "achiever." To admit failure may be more embarrassing or humiliating than the adolescent can tolerate.

Adolescents will sometimes lie to live up to a reputation based on a past record of performance or on peer standards (no matter how misguided). Consider, for example, the classic example of boys who brag to their male peers about "scoring" with girls. A boy who does this often hopes to enhance his image of being the "cool" one. Thus he also can cover fears of sexual involvement, fears of appearing awkward and inexperienced with girls, or of being rejected by girls, and even fears of impotence. Lying about sexual "scoring" in such instances is a plausible, if not wholly admirable, way of salvaging self-respect when the truth might expose the teen-ager to ridicule and feelings of failure.

Recently I worked with a 15-year-old whose lying had become part of an elaborate performance she would put on to attract the attention of her class-mates. This young lady would appear to faint pe-riodically following episodes of hyperventilation. When questioned in the nurse's office, she explained that her family doctor had diagnosed her fainting spells as symptoms of a terminal disease which gave her less than a year to live. Although a phone call to the girl's mother quickly proved beyond a doubt that this story was not true, the girl continued to spread work of her imminent death among those of her classmates who were not aware of the truth. As a result of this story, she was able to attract consid-erable attention for a time and become something of a "celebrity."*

As seen from the few examples I've presented, lies by teen-agers are usually misguided attempts to deal with a problem or an unpleasant situation. The more problems that a teen-ager has and is not solv-ing successfully, the more apt he is to resort to tell-ing lies. Unfortunately, lying doesn't work; it simply tends to build up an ever-expanding cycle of prob-lems. The scenario is often like this:

A) Parents ask the child where he is going.
B) The child lies. (Lie No. 1.)
C) The parents know better, and confront the child.
D) The child lies again to cover Lie No. 1. (Now we have Lie No. 2.)

*This kind of lying to one's peers is always cause for concern, because it can indicate a deep underlying disturbance. If a teen-ager persists in using lies as a routine way of relating to one's peers, it may be a symptom of problems that ought to be discussed with a professional therapist. The danger here is that such habitual social liars often tend to believe their own lies about themselves, blurring fantasy with reality. Lying to oneself in this manner is a serious matter that should be attended to.

E) Punishment by the parents.

F) The child associates punishment with being caught in a lie. (Prepares for Lie No. 3.)

And so it goes. Lying, unhappily, breaks down trust and drives a wedge between a teen-ager and his parents, between a teen-ager and his peers and between a teen-ager and the adult community. A child who lies is under suspicion, his life is under surveillance, he is something of an outcast because he is not trusted. He has, in short, worked himself into a serious bind.

How to Deal with Teen-age Lying

From what we have seen it should begin to be clear that teen-age lying is not something that exists in the abstract. The lying is intrinsically connected to underlying behavior problems. It is my view that you cannot deal with the problem of lying without dealing with the circumstances in the life of a teen-ager that make him feel he has to lie. You cannot simply tell a teen-ager that it is "wrong" to lie, or even that it works against his own best interests when he lies. If he is behaving, in the first place, in a way that is likely to get him into trouble, it is unrealistic to expect that, in the second place, he will turn to his parents, or any other adult, and say, "Oh, by the way, I'm doing something wrong." This simply won't happen. The child who does something that he knows is wrong, or that he believes will be perceived as wrong, is not going to go out of his way to send out *truth bulletins* about it. He is going to lie.

The key to reaching a teen-ager who is a persistent liar (the term that the "authorities" like to use is "pathological" liar) is to help him solve those problems that make him feel he has to lie, thereby creating an *environment of behavioral success* for him that will make lying unnecessary.

Let's look at the example of the teen-ager who withholds a report card from his parents, forges their names to it and returns it to the school. When the parents learn about what has happened, in the majority of cases they will be shocked and angry that their child has done such a thing.

The typical reaction is: "My child will grow up to be a check forger and end up in the penitentiary."

What often gets overlooked in such instances is the question of why did the child feel obliged to do what he did in the first place?

Is the child "goofing off" in school? If so, what's behind it?

Is the allure of associating with his peers more compelling to the child than the sterility of the classroom? What can be done about this?

Is it possible that the child has a learning disability that should be attended to?

Is there trouble at home that is interfering with the child's concentration?

Is the child being pushed to accomplish more than he or she can handle right now?

Is punitive action for a poor report likely to be so harsh that the child is simply afraid to tell the truth?

In the circumstances under consideration, these are key questions that need to be asked, understood and cleared up. I am firmly convinced that the way to deal with teen-age lying is, first and foremost, to find out why the child felt compelled to do what he did that was wrong, and then help him in that behavior area so that he doesn't have to do the same thing again, thereby *removing any further need* to lie. The case study that follows provides an example of this process and how it can be developed.

CASE STUDY—CAROLYN P.

The Complaint

Seventeen-year-old Carolyn P. was referred to me through her high school guidance department. As is so often the case in such referrals, only six months before Carolyn had been an honor student, but was now receiving mostly C's and D's, and in two subject her interim grades were F. Moreover, she had been suspended from the high school marching band on one occasion (for one week) for having boarded a school bus with alcohol in her possession. On another recent occasion she had been sent to the principal's office for smoking marijuana in the senior lounge. Her interim grade report mentioned numerous "cuts" in classes.

At our first session with Carolyn and her parents, Mr. and Mrs. P. also enumerated several other incidents that had taken place recently. Carolyn had been caught drinking liquor in a supermarket parking lot, and her name had been taken by the police. She was developing a habit of "disappearing" from her home early in the evenings and not telling her parents where she was going, or even that she was leaving. It had since been confirmed that she had been going to parties and participating in drinking beer.

What upset Mr. and Mrs. P. most was the fact that when confronted with all of these matters Carolyn had lied. Only after irrefutable evidence had been presented to her had she admitted what was already known.

Mr. P. was the more unforgiving of the two parents, and stated in the presence of all of us at our first therapy session that he had "lost trust" in Carolyn because of her "bad decisions" and because of her attempted lying cover-ups. As a result of her "blatant disrespect" for her parents, Mr. P. just prior to our first therapy session had delivered an ultimatum to Carolyn: Either she was to abide by her parents' rules or leave the house and live somewhere else.

If the threat to forbid Carolyn to live at home was designed to frighten her, it was not well considered. She had already left home for two days on one occasion, and upon returning had stated that she felt it was "good getting away." Her response to charges by her parents that she was going to beer parties and hanging out with, in her mother's words, "less than terrific folk," was that her parents were "overly restrictive." Carolyn's mother seemed to have a foreboding sense of the consequences of the conflict that existed between her daughter and Mr. P. At one point she said, "My fear is that we're on a collision course; that Carolyn will leave home for good if we don't reach some kind of compromise."

Background

The situation was not quite as hopeless, however, as everyone at the first session seemed to believe. For one thing, although Mr. and Mrs. P. had placed considerable emphasis on Carolyn's recent problem behavior, they tended to overlook for the moment some of their daughter's more positive traits and accomplishments. As the eldest child, with two younger brothers, ages 13 and 11, Carolyn had always been, in her father's own words, the "standard bearer" among the children until the recent rash of accidents. Not only had she been an honor roll student, even now as therapy was commencing she was working 15 hours a week at a local pet shop and was baby-sitting in the neighborhood. Although all of the children in the family were bright, Carolyn had been singled out as "Daddy's girl" and the "brain" of the family.

As we progressed, certain information emerged that helped explain Mr. P.'s strong feelings with regard to his daughter's behavior. Mr. P.'s own mother had been an alcoholic and had died prematurely of cirrhosis of the liver when Mr. P. was an adolescent. Moreover, his older sister, who had then become his guardian, later developed into a hard drug user, and as a result of her addiction had been in and out of institutions over a long period of years.

Having grown up in an atmosphere of self-destructive alcohol and drug abuse, Mr. P. was especially concerned lest his daughter end up following along the same path. Mr. P.'s fears and his strong negative attitude toward alcohol and drugs conflicted with Carolyn's own feelings that there was "nothing wrong" with going out with her friends and "doing what everybody does." She confided to us that until she had started going to parties and having "a beer now and then" she had felt that she was an "automaton" and a "boring person." Clearly, she had reached a point in life where her role as "Daddy's girl" could no longer be taken for granted.

Reaching Understanding

What helped this family reach an understanding and a compromise solution was that both parents and daughter really did want to end the current conflict. Although Carolyn was strong-willed and going through a discovery period of liberating herself from the role of family "standard bearer," there was something solid remaining, as there so often is in such situations, that held her back from rejecting her parents completely. Obviously, Carolyn's parents wanted accommodation or they wouldn't have sought out therapeutic help in the first place. Mrs. P. said she was "more sad than angry" that Carolyn seemed to desire to avoid the family in favor of her new friends. "Maybe," Mrs. P. said, "we ought to accept the fact that Carolyn needs to be more her own person."

In this ameliorative atmosphere, Carolyn felt free enough to volunteer some information that for the first time addressed directly her parents' fears about her drinking and drug use.

"I don't go out and get drunk!" Carolyn said with some emotion at one of our sessions. "I think drinking too much is *stupid*. Maybe I went too far on one or two occasions. But I've learned how to balance myself. I don't go out to *drink*. I go out to be with my friends, and I take maybe one beer. I'm not ashamed of anything I've done. I feel better about myself since I started being a part of the group I hang out with than I did before when I was a boring little wimp!"

Carolyn seemed to be reassuring her parents that she was not the alcoholic or drug addict that they had feared, and immediately her father jumped in with what turned out to be a *pivotal concession*. Mr. P. said he *didn't mind Carolyn drinking in moderation* if he knew where she was at the time, rather than doing it *behind his back*.

It was then that the root cause underlying Carolyn's lying came out. As a result of her father's experience with his mother and sister she had known all her life how he felt about drinking and drugs. Yes, she had experimented with "pot" a couple of times with a couple of other girls in the senior lounge. (She confessed she was "not crazy about it.") She admitted that she had shown poor judgment carrying a bottle onto the school bus and drinking publicly in the supermarket parking lot, but she had only been trying to "break out" of her old self-image, and was letting the other kids know she was one of the gang. She had lied to her parents and to the school authorities about these incidents because she had been "afraid" of how her father would react to it all.

"I was right, too," she added, turning to her father. "You went up the wall."

The tears that suddenly were rolling down Mr. P.'s cheeks were not out of sadness, but out of relief that his daughter really was the "solid citizen" that he had always believed her to be, even though she was changing some of her ways in the process of developing into a young woman.

Creative Synthesis

With a clear explanation of their respective fears and desires presented, Mr. and Mrs. P. and Carolyn set about to negotiate a resolution of their differences. Mr. P. announced that he would "compromise," allowing Carolyn to drink in moderation at neighborhood parties if she would leave the telephone number of where she would be, and promise not to ride in a car with anyone who had been drinking.

Carolyn readily agreed to these terms. She had some complaints of her own to air, however. Her parents were "too rigid," she said, about not allowing her to smoke cigarettes and forbidding her to use nail polish and hair coloring. Here, again, a compromise was reached, although like most compromises, not everyone was overly thrilled. Mr. and Mrs. P. said, yes, Carolyn could use whatever nail polish and hair coloring she wanted to use, but they felt she was much prettier "without all that paint, eye liner and dye." As far as smoking was concerned, Mr. P., a former three-packs-a-day smoker who had managed after many years to quit, absolutely forbade smoking in the house. He even went so far as to say he would not condone Carolyn's smoking *anywhere*, but he then relented to the extent of stating that if his daughter smoked outside the house "and I don't hear about it, I won't make a federal case of it." From a former heavy smoker who was personally aware of the destructive aspects of cigarette smoking, this was a fair compromise.

With all points laid out clearly for all to see, and with an agreement reached, there remained only a period of time to pass to see how it would work out. At a suitable later date I talked with Mrs. P. who informed me that Carolyn was acting more responsibly in every area, and, particularly, when she went to parties she was leaving telephone numbers which could be verified. Her studying was more consistent, and her grades were showing a dramatic improvement. As far as lying was concerned, Mrs. P. said, "I can't think of any reason why she would want to lie to us now."

Practical Steps

The case of Carolyn P. illustrates clearly the point that I have been making: If your child is lying, there is an underlying reason for it that needs attention.

At the age of 17 Carolyn P. was beginning to experiment with beer and a couple of puffs of marijuana. For the first time in her life she was beginning to feel "grown up" and popular with her group.

For reasons of his own, having to do with a family history of alcohol and drug abuse, Carolyn's father understandably had already made it known that he would not condone the use of either alcohol or drugs by his daughter, even on an infrequent experimental basis. To avoid a direct and ugly confrontation with her father, Carolyn had resorted to lying to anyone whom she thought might report her activities to her parents.

Once Carolyn's parents were able to understand that their daughter was not falling into a life of debauchery and self-destructive alcohol and drug use, they were able to compromise their own rather rigid standards, and set up new rules of behavior that were acceptable to everyone. The lying ceased.

There are lessons for parents in the case of this teen-ager whose lying was a misguided attempt to avoid parental disapproval.

I. Look behind the lie

A child lies to cover up something that either is wrong or that he believes others will *think* is wrong. In either case, the lie is an intricate part of prior behavior. The child has not yet learned that lying probably will create more problems for him in the long run than if he were to come right out and tell the truth.

Lies usually are not difficult to detect. Sooner or later they reveal themselves. At the point when they do, parents should try to focus not so much on the fact of the lie itself, but more on why the child did what he did that necessitated telling the lie.

Perhaps it will help to think of a teen-age lie as a *signal* that something else is going on. Don't ignore the signal, but don't concentrate on it to the exclusion of what's behind it, either. A flashing red light at a railroad crossing means a train is coming. You pay attention to the signal, but you are really on the look-out for the train. The signal your child is flashing at you through a lie is no less of a sign that there is something else to be aware of further down the track.

II. Talk to your child

After your first feelings of hurt, outrage and surprise that your child would lie to you, get down to the business of trying to understand what is going on that necessitated the lie. It might not be a bad idea to start out by asking yourself a few questions first. Is your child attempting to define new directions for himself that he is afraid you will criticize if he tells the truth? Is he having such large problems in his peer relationships that he is afraid to talk directly about them? Is it possible your child is afraid of harsh punishment from you if he tells you what's really on his mind? Is it possible you should renegotiate some of the family rules that may be too strict?

Explore with your teen-ager any hunches you may have as to what's behind your child's lying. Try to find out what your child is really thinking. Remember, exploring areas of concern with your teen-ager is not the same as *talking at* your teen-ager. Don't lecture! Don't set up a heavy confrontation scene. Listen carefully to what your child is trying to tell you. Listening carefully may require that you listen *between the lines*. Very often your child will tell you what's on his mind, though it may come out in dribs and drabs and in a very roundabout way. It may take a bit of deciphering. It may take a bit of patience, as well.

III. Don't be punitive

When you have caught your child in a lie your first reaction may be that punishment is called for. The most common punishment is "grounding," or taking away a privilege of some kind. Don't resort to these tactics! A threat of punishment is the surest way of encouraging your child to lie every time. If your child knows that you are critical and judging him harshly, he will tell you as little of what you need to know as possible. Your task is to win your child's trust. You can't do this if you drive him away with criticism and punishment.

IV. Examine your own values

Adolescence is a time of experimentation. How else is a teen-ager to find out where he is strongest and where weakest if he doesn't explore new directions? It can almost be guaranteed that the healthy teen-age child will at one time or another test himself in areas that you, as an adult from another generation, may not wholly approve of.

Believe it or not, your teen-ager knows you better than you think he does. Remember how surprised you were the first time your teen-ager in a light family moment mimicked one of your dinner table mannerisms that you had not realized was apparent? Teen-agers may not know themselves, but they know *you*. And they know what you approve of, and what you don't approve of. You don't even have to tell them. When they are about to experiment with new directions in life, they know exactly what your attitude will be. If your child feels that your attitudes and beliefs are a little bit "neanderthal" insofar as current peer behavior patterns are concerned, he almost certainly will be evasive rather than let you know what he is doing.

The questions you should ask yourself are: Are you too rigid in some of your fixed positions? Is your child forced to lie to you to *protect* you from hurt feelings? Is he *afraid* to share with you some of the normal experiences of teen-age growth and experimentation because of the way he knows that you will react? If so, perhaps you should open up the subject with him of negotiating new rules that you both can live with. In the case of girls, particularly, parents should ask themselves if they are up on current attitudes concerning dating and sexual matters. (See Problem #9: What About My Kid and Sex?)

V. Teen-age lying is not a "federal case"

In the story of the little shepherd boy who cried "Wolf!" we noted earlier that lying is one of society's strictest taboos. There should be a difference, however, between parents today and the villagers of the shepherd's town. The villagers consigned their little kid to the hungry stomach of the wolf. Hopefully, in a more enlightened society parents will recognize that a cry of "Wolf!" can be a signal that needs further exploration.

It is important to remember, I think, that the adolescent who feels compelled to tell a lie is not some kind of sub-human species. The lie is simply an indication that the child has not found a way of coping successfully in some particular area of his life. Precisely because he is young and inexperienced he takes what appears to be a course that will provide the easiest way out. He has yet to learn that the "easiest" course more often than not turns out to be the harder course. It is our job as caring parents not to treat a teen-age lie as a "federal case," but to help our children realize that there is a better way.

If you can convince your teen-ager that you are more interested in helping him to resolve the underlying problem behind the lie than you are concerned about the fact of the lie itself, you may find that the next time, instead of telling you a lie, your teen-ager will open up and tell you what is on his mind. At the point when this happens you will know that you have taken a giant step in helping your youngster appreciate one of the most valuable moral lessons he will ever learn: Life works better when you are able to tell the truth.

Problem #4

///

"My Kid Goes Around Being Bored All the Time"

Do you remember the time when your seventh grader son hit a home run with the bases loaded in Little League? Or the time when your daughter in sixth grade played Cinderella in the class play? What wonderful times those were, when all the world seemed to stand still for a few precious moments and you were filled with happiness and wonderment.

There were other wonderful times, too. Such a happy family you all were, lucky enough to spend time together in the country, swimming together in an abandoned quarry, identifying local birds or wild flowers, picking wild strawberries. (The kids gobbled theirs down, leaving red smears on their lips and cheeks.)

Who would have believed that children in a family such as this could ever be *bored*?

And yet, now, only a few short years later, on a beautiful Sunday afternoon in June, you find that same son, now 15 years old, lying flat on his back on his bed, his eyes focused vaguely on nothing up there in the vicinity of the ceiling. Though he is reclining, his body is not relaxed; as his longtime parent you can sense a tension in his limbs. (Perhaps it is the absence of the blaring sound of rock music from the stereo that is the real tip-off that things are not as they ought to be.)

Down the hall, your 13-year-old daughter is on her bed, too. She has propped herself up against a pile of frilly pillows and stuffed teddy bears. She snaps her gum while leafing impatiently through the pages of a teen-age girl's magazine. She does not look happy.

The conversation with either child predictably goes along these lines.

"Hi. What's up?" From experience you know enough about teen-age moodiness to feel your way cautiously.

"Nothing."

"How come you're not out catching some rays?"

No answer. A shrug.

"Anything wrong?"

"No."

"I thought you were going on a picnic today with some of your friends."

"It's too boring."

"Boring? I thought you—"

"It's all boring. Everything is boring around here."

Immediately you try to think of ways to relieve the situation, or condition. "Do you want me to drive you anywhere?"

"No."

It is very frustrating, and you find that you are getting angry.

"Maybe if you got up off that bed and tried to do something for yourself you wouldn't feel so bored." Even a fight, which this kind of comment could very well provoke, is better than the pathetic hopeless aspect their boredom presents.

"I just want to be left alone."

And there it is. More than anger, suddenly you feel depressed. Your kid maybe has talked back to you in the past, but this apparent turning his back on life itself has never happened before. Suddenly it is not only a question of being pained or annoyed at seeing this attractive, bright and otherwise charming young person in a state of near torpor. There is a new feeling on your part of helplessness and even of fear.

How could this have occurred? What happened to the children's interest in reading and culture and sports and the great outdoors? Where and when did they suddenly go wrong? Where did *you* go wrong? How can kids that have so much to offer waste it all by being bored?

Why Kids Are Bored

Among all creatures in the animal kingdom, man is uniquely capable of boredom. Other animals spend their time hunting for food, hunting for a mate with which to procreate the species, or sleeping. Because human beings are required to spend only a portion of their time at survival functions, they have *spare time* on their hands. They have to think up ways to amuse themselves or they suffer from that existential anomie—boredom.

All people are bored from time to time. Adults, however, are not devastated by short periods of boredom. They have had experience with it; they have learned that life is not always an exciting smorgasbord of entertaining alternatives served up on a silver platter. They know that life cannot be exciting *all the time*.

The difference between teen-age boredom and adult boredom is simply that teen-agers do not know that occasional boredom is a natural and inescapable part of life. The teen-age years are a time of *great expectations*. And teen-agers are, of course, impatient. They want to grab onto the future—now. Unfortunately, the reality of life, as we adults know so well, does not often keep pace with youthful expectations. The resultant absence of challenge or stimulation is the phenomenon we know as boredom. Lacking the experience to deal with existential boredom, teen-agers suffer more. In their generally impatient frame of mind, a few moments of boredom can seem like an eternity. As a result, they are likely to exhibit symptoms of irritability, grouchiness, lassitude, and a tendency to do nothing but lie about and simply blame the rest of the world for being the root cause of their present unhappy state. A funny paradox is at work. During all those pre-teen years they looked to you to entertain them; now, in their eagerness to be on their own, they do not want your help. At the same time, not understanding and not knowing who else to blame, they blame you for not providing the means by which they can be stimulated.

Exacerbating this situation greatly today are the influences exerted on teen-agers, and pre-teen-agers, by the consumerist culture in which we live. Young people are bombarded by promotional messages through the media of television, advertising, movies, rock videos, video cassette recorders, and even print. Our highly promotion-oriented world has set up the unrealistic expectation among today's teen kids that they must be occupied, stimulated, challenged every moment. (After all, you can't sell surfboards and soft drinks to kids who are in their rooms contemplating the meaning of the universe.) Advertising tells kids how to dress, what to do, and how to behave. Since the image is the message (i.e., looking "cool," riding in a sports car, picking up the sexiest, happiest, and best-looking partner available), anything that falls short of these images, and the implied promises they portray, is likely to produce feelings of boredom.

As a consequence of this media exposure, the experience of boredom has proliferated and intensified, I believe, among today's teen-agers. When expectations of fulfillment surpass the possible content of certain experiences, the person feels bored.

In this context of super-heated expectations, teen-age kids also must face the real-life challenge of passing from childhood into adulthood. They are poised on the threshhold of a wide variety of important life choices, whether to go to college, whether to work for Dad, whether to live away from home or remain close by. It is a place where the future can appear to be extremely forbidding. Having given up most childhood pleasures, teen-agers suddenly find themselves at a point when they must move forward, but at the same time when they peer into the future they see very little that is friendly and familiar to move forward into. Over and over they have been told how great they are. (Remember that Little League home run; the part in the Cinderella play.) Unsure, maybe even doubting if they will ever define for themselves a clear direction for future activity, not to mention other more delicate areas such as finding compatibility with the opposite sex, teen-agers are prone to experience confusion and indecisiveness. Is it any wonder that many teen-agers have a tendency to draw back for a time from taking part in those activities that normally you could expect them to be a part of? Very often they experience this temporary withdrawal as boredom—boredom with life, with themselves, and with those who would most like to help.

Closely allied to this indecisiveness about the future is the boredom expressed by teen-agers who simply are afraid of *right now*. Adolescents are extremely sensitive to the opinions of their peers. A teen-ager who is shy, for example, may be afraid, afraid of participating in a new activity, of making new friends, or of simply breaking well-established patterns of behavior. If your teen-ager complains of boredom while resisting calling up friends and participating in other social activities, it very well may be that he is engaging in a form of human hibernation that protects him from social failure. Saying that so-and-so is "boring" may actually be a way of rejecting that other person before that person rejects him. This attitude may also help to salvage self-esteem by elevating oneself above others.

When kids complain that school is boring, it may simply be because they are not performing well. Similarly, if a child comes back from a tennis lesson complaining that it was boring, it may be because he or she has been unable to perform with any degree of adeptness.*

Some teen-agers who appear to be bored may be reacting to a situation of over-control or exaggerated dominance by one or both parents. Kids who are permitted only the smallest measure of autonomy at home may complain the most strenuously about boredom. In such instances, the teen-ager usually is carrying within him a great deal of anger about the restrictive environment in which he lives. His boredom may be simply the only permissible manifestation of his real feeling, which is anger. In such instances of suppressed resentment we are likely to find a lack of motivation with regard to one's homework, or endless procrastination in doing chores for the family. The unconscious aim is to anger one's parents through passive-aggressive behav-

*Some children are bored by school *not* because they are not capable of performing, but because they are extremely bright, and their abilities are beyond what is being offered in the curriculum. Many school districts now make efforts to place high achieving children into classes with other high achievers. Similarly, in sports, tennis is not for everyone, and the child who cannot perform on the courts may be talented in other areas where he can excel.

ior, a pattern usually perceived as "laziness" by the parents.

Like adults, teen-agers make efforts, of course, to combat boredom. Some teen-agers are able to make modifications in their normal routines that will relieve boredom. They will call a friend and chat on the phone, or go to the movies, or join in a pick-up handball or basketball game, or get a tennis match. Other teen-agers, partly because of their inflated expectations and along with this a demand for escape, will try to relieve their boredom through destructive means, as, for example, engaging in excessive pot smoking, or drinking, or driving too fast, or promiscuous sex. There is a difference in all of these activities, but there is a similarity, too: the striving to eliminate boredom through having fun.

Sometimes teen-agers and other young adults seek a remedy for boredom by latching onto a noble cause. Because they are idealistic and believe that life should be better than it is, they join political movements or religious groups and support or even initiate opposition to perceived social injustice in a grand effort to make life measure up to their ideals. These youngsters while finding ways of relieving boredom oftentimes are making a contribution to a better world. In a similar manner, kids who are talented athletes or possess artistic or creative talent and who have the desire to work at developing their skills are fortunate to find meaningful outlets for their abundance of free-floating energy.

One note of caution: Although occasional boredom is a natural rite of passage which is to be expected, prolonged boredom accompanied by depression may signal a dangerous condition that should not be ignored. If your child is reacting in a bored and depressed way following the death of a loved one, or to the death of a school acquaintance as the result of an accident, or worse, suicide, attention should be paid. If your child continuously utters the complaint, "I'm bored," the complaint should be looked at as possibly something more than just boredom. It could be that such a teenager is attempting to protect himself from additional assaults on his stability. Indeed, when a youngster complains of an inner emptiness, talks about suicide, or manifests a general withdrawal over a protracted period of time, professional intervention is a *must*. Although suicidal behavior is complicated and enigmatic, there are danger signals which a professional can usually pinpoint. If there is any doubt in your mind about whether or not your child may possibly be suicidal, it would be better to seek reassurance from a professional than to ignore it.

Coping with the Bored Teen-ager

Watching your teen-ager mope around the house in a state of the doldrums is not only trying, but worrisome. One common approach is to try to make things better no matter what sacrifice is required. Another approach is to react with anger and accusations. Before suggesting some practical steps you might try in dealing with your bored teenager, let's take a look at a couple of case histories.

CASE STUDY I—WILLY N.

The Complaint

The case of Willy N. is one that is particularly interesting because it involved a somewhat unconventional approach, one that took considerable courage on the part of his mother. At our first meeting Willy was accompanied by his mother. It was an odd sight, the two of them. Willy looked like a creature from the backwoods—husky, with wisps of whiskers on his otherwise smooth chin, and he was wearing faded jeans with scuffed motorcycle boots, and a bedraggled T-shirt with the death's head emblem of some outrageous rock band on the front and the back. Willy's mother, on the other hand, was slight of build and wore a neat pants suit.

"I tried to get him to put on a decent shirt, but he wouldn't" was Mrs. N.'s opening remark.

That was just the beginning of a list of complaints that read almost like a sheet from a police report. Among her complaints was that he smoked too much pot, hung out at the supermarket parking lot, doing "God knows what," was irresponsible and untrustworthy, and was always cursing at his younger brother and sister. She saved the most serious item for last: "He's tired all the time, and won't get up and go to school. He probably won't graduate next June, and won't be able to go to college!"

I expected Willy to become defensive and to go into a tirade at his mother, but on the contrary, he simply said, "I'm tired because my subjects are boring, and I can't wait to get out." He went on to say that he didn't want to be bored, but "I can't help it; it's a waste of time."

"Do you want to graduate and go to college?" I asked him.

He shrugged. "I guess so. Mom wants me to."

In later sessions, when his mother was not present, Willy seemed mildly depressed and anxiously confused. He described himself as "lost and bewildered." Assuming he would be able to graduate from high school, choices for the future seemed wide open. He had no direction.

Willy felt out of place in almost every environment except the one he shared with a sub-group of his peers. School was a bore, and home was an irritant. His brother and sister were "nerds." Town was the worst, because everybody seemed "old" and intolerant of kids like himself.

Any notions he had of his future revolved around fantasies of being either a professional superstar athlete (though he would take no part in organized school sports), or an heir to a huge fortune, living a life of leisure on beachfront property, or becoming an explorer such as Jacques Cousteau. The reality of Willy's existence, which his mother had described fairly accurately, was a far distance from these high expectations.

One thing about Willy intrigued me. He loved to draw, and in fact he spent much of the time during our sessions scratching on a notepad. The drawings that he showed me were bold depictions of grotesque faces or weaponry, drawings that suggested anger and derision. I also learned that Willy liked to read and even to write poetry. His favorite fiction stories portrayed a hero overcoming seemingly insurmountable odds. His favorite lines of poetry were the lyrics of alienated rock groups.

Background

The eldest of three children, Willy was 17 and a first semester high school senior when we first met. He had a 16-year old brother and a 14-year-old sister, both of whom were doing well in school. Willy's parents had divorced two years previously, leaving Mrs. N. with full custody of the children. Mr. N. had remarried, and was living out of town.

Although I never met Mr. N., Mrs. N. described him as a "high-powered" advertising executive. He had been a track star in college, and he had always been successful at anything he tried to do. Willy and the other children all spent some vacation time with Mr. N., but Willy felt totally out of place with his father, whose no-nonsense businessman approach to life was inescapably linked in Willy's mind with the attitude of the "boring and intolerant" townspeople. Although Mr. N. did not approve of Willy's lifestyle, he did not attempt to influence him (probably wisely), and the relationship, such as it was, was described by Willy as "a Mexican standoff." Although Willy felt that he did not want to follow in the footsteps of his father, at the same time he admitted that he would like to surpass his father in some career of his own choice.

Mrs. N. had always wanted to go to college, but being one of six children from a lower middle class family, she had to go to work instead. She felt that anyone who did not go to college was missing out on something important, and she even implied that if she had gone to college she and her husband "might have had more in common and would still be together." She exhibited considerable depression over the possibility that Willy would flunk out of high school and not be able to go on for a higher education.

Reaching Understanding

From looking at the several different points of view of the various people involved, it soon became clear why Willy was feeling "lost and bewildered."

Willy was a boy with a lot of unrealized creative talent and energy. At the same time, he had not yet reached the point where he knew the direction he was going to take. School did not stimulate his interests, and, pointing to his father as an example, Willy didn't believe that college would be much better. On the other hand, it bothered him that he should appear to be a failure in his father's eyes, and it genuinely saddened him not to satisfy his mother's wish for him to get a higher education. The long and short of it was that Willy was very conflicted. Feeling helpless no matter in which direction he turned, his escape was to turn off the entire reality of his life and drift into a fantasy world of high living and superstardom

Creative Synthesis

After several months of working with Willy I concluded that in the near term, before he could emerge from the doldrums, his mother would have to change some of her own thinking first.

The three of us met, and I pointed out that although Willy was a big husky fellow (with that wisp of whiskers), his development insofar as what he wanted to do with his life was lagging behind his physical development. I said that though it might be difficult for Mrs. N. to accept, some children simply are not as ready as others to take the next step forward onto the ladder of life. Perhaps Willy was one of those kids who should wait awhile before trying to make a college commitment. I pointed out to Mrs. N. that Willy's boredom and the associated unproductive pursuits he was engaged in were manifestations of his attempt to escape, to go into hibernation, until such time as this bitterly conflicted period in his life should pass and he could step out once again into a world that would present itself in a friendlier and warmer and clearer light. Willy, I said, should be encouraged right now to follow his own best instincts.

It took some courage, I believe, but one week later, just prior to Willy's next meeting with me, Mrs. N. called, and told me that she and Willy had had "a good talk," and that they had agreed that Willy should *drop out of his last term of high school and take a job until the following September.* Certainly this was an extreme step, but under the circumstances, I believe it was one that made sense. Willy was going to fail, in any case. By making a conscious choice to leave school until a later time, he was stepping out of his mood of indifference, and was taking charge of his own life for the first time in months.

And what was the result of this radical step? In the weeks that followed, Willy got a job working at a gas station five days a week. He actually felt triumphant about having his first full-time job. It seemed to relax him. He made it clear he was going to take better care of his body in the future, and he immediately cut down on his pot smoking and organized a regimen of daily exercises. It pleased him, I was happy to learn, that his mother, having postponed her ambitions for him to enter college, was suddenly less depressed. Most important, Willy said the thing that "bored" him the most right now was "cruising around" with the old gang at the supermarket. After a time, Willy and I agreed that we could terminate treatment. Fourteen months later he called me one afternoon to tell me that he had just graduated from high school! He had re-enrolled the following spring term, and had passed his course "in a breeze." He already had made application for admittance to a state college where he hoped to pursue his interest in art.

CASE STUDY II—ROBERT G.

The Complaint

If the case of Willy N. represents one end of the spectrum—that is, the young man who rejects conventional "straight" society—the case of Robert G. represents the other end—that of the teen-ager whose life is made boring because he is unable to find acceptance. Robert, a skinny 13-year-old with a distrustful expression, was referred to me by his school guidance counselor who expressed the view that the boy was "alienated from his peers."

Alienated, it turned out, was a mild word; Robert was actually the object of many childhood pranks and much ridicule. Because of his lack of confidence and his general hang-dog demeanor, he tended to mumble and swallow his words, thus hiding the fact, even from his teachers, that he was quite bright. He was not getting good grades in his classes.

Although keenly aware of not fitting in with the

crowd, Robert feigned not to care. In fact, he boasted about being a "true individual," neither a "jock," nor "brain," nor "freak," nor "preppy," which effectively included just about everybody. He complained that his peers were all "boring." What bored him the most, he stated, was the ritual that the other kids followed of "going to town." "Hanging out" was boring. Thus, as a result of either excluding himself or being excluded from all social distractions, Robert's life shuttled between school, which he found boring, and home, which also was boring. He was, in fact, mildly depressed.

Background

Robert had some rather compelling reasons to be bored at home. His parents were both connected to the movie industry, and were absent much of the time. Mrs. G. was an independent producer of documentary films, and Mr. G. owned and operated several movie theatres. Both were rather flamboyant and colorful characters, and Robert was somewhat in awe of them. Unfortunately, they both were very busy pursuing their careers, and it was rare that he even saw them except on week-ends. His only companion at home was the housekeeper who cooked his meals.

As an only child and with his parents mostly absent, Robert confessed that he felt like an orphan. And like many orphans, he tended to feel (it came out in time) that he was unlovable and somewhat unattractive and uninteresting.

"They don't care about me," Robert said. And that seemed to be the way he looked upon the whole world.

In point of fact, Robert's parents cared about him very much, and it pained them to see him suffering so much social ostracism, particularly because they themselves were extremely popular and attended many glamorous film-world functions. In order to compensate for her frequent absences and in a seeming effort to pump some enthusiasm into her son, Mrs. G. tended to be overbearing toward Robert when she saw him. She would suggest a half dozen things he should do to "fit into the crowd," all of which, of course, he would reject, much to her disappointment.

Mr. G., on the other hand, tended when he was home to throw himself into a strenuous routine of lawn and garden work, occasionally ordering Robert to "do this or do that," which Robert did without much outward complaining, but with much inner resentment.

Reaching Understanding

As Robert's boredom and depression persisted, I attempted to be supportive by suggesting steps that he might take to move a bit into the mainstream of life. This was a mistake, as I quickly learned when he accused me of behaving exactly like "the family director," his mother. I had to admit that he was right. Later when we settled into a weekly routine of playing chess and engaging in small talk, therapy progressed a bit. The non-threatening nature of casual conversations helped reduce some of Robert's social anxiety around me.

It finally came out that for him to call a friend and be turned down was tantamount to death. He really was *very angry* about not fitting in with his peers. Boredom was a protective device he had erected to prevent himself from being hurt. What he needed, I concluded, was a bit of confidence that he could succeed in a social situation.

To help Robert gain confidence, his parents needed to change some of their ways of relating to him. Mrs. G.'s efforts to get Robert to "come out of his shell" were actually *serving to reinforce the negative feelings he had about himself.* By trying to direct his life in an overbearing manner she was actually undermining his confidence to do things for himself. On the other hand, his father's brusque matter-of-fact way of ordering Robert about reinforced Robert's feeling that his father didn't care about him.

Creative Synthesis

In a meeting between the four of us, I stated to the parents that I firmly believed that Robert's current problems were largely the result of growing pains that he would eventually outgrow. The parents were relieved that their son did not "hate" them, or that he was some kind of "hopeless case."

Having opened the discussion with those remarks, I then revealed to Mrs. G. the initial antagonism that Robert had felt toward *me* when I had tried to direct him into particular activities. Mrs. G. smiled as she recognized a familiar pattern with Robert. It was an easy step then for her to agree to stop trying to direct Robert's life and allow him to progress at his own pace. She confessed that she probably had been "overcompensating" for being away from home so much. She said she thought that in the future she would be able to show her love and interest in Robert without overwhelming him with direction.

To her husband, I gave a diametrically opposed message. Robert needed a male role model, someone to play chess with and "shoot the breeze with," if you like. I urged him to make an effort to spend more time with Robert, time that would be leisurely, not just working and ordering about. Mr. G. immediately agreed to find more time to spend with Robert. I was pleased to observe in the weeks that followed that he managed to be at home at least two nights a week by six P.M., at which time he and Robert went out to a restaurant for dinner together.

As summer vacation approached, I felt it was a crucial period for Robert; I was worried that there would be even more free time for him during which he might feel alone and neglected. But his parents were now tuned in to his needs. His mother, playing a very low-key, behind-the-scenes role, arranged for him to interview for a job as messenger at her production company in New York City. Well, what do you know? He got the job. During that summer he met a variety of people, including some actors whom he liked and who *liked him*. He traveled the subways on his own, delivering messages. He earned some money for his bank account, and he made a point of going to several stage plays and a lot of movies.

I could hardly believe my eyes when I saw him again for continued treatment in the fall. During the summer, he had grown almost two inches, and his voice was beginning to change. The changes, both inner and outward, continued during the school year. Robert got involved in the school theatre group, and played a major part in the school play.

(He was good, too; I was there opening night.) With his new success, his confidence began to grow. His grades jumped from a C to a B-plus average. A playful side of his personality that had been hidden before began to emerge. And even his posture improved.

By the spring term, he had grown another *three inches*; he looked like any other normal teen-ager. He went to his first rock concert with a couple of his new theatre club friends. (They smoked pot, which he told me he didn't like.) By now he was feeling his oats and growing mildly restive about the weekly therapy involvement. At *his* suggestion, we agreed to meet every two weeks on an experimental basis. Therapy was terminated a week before school ended in June.

Practical Steps

Although Willy N. and Robert G. were bored for different reasons, there was in both cases a similar underlying cause. For both boys life was not measuring up to expectations; they felt helpless and confused. Since they couldn't *grab* on to the merry-go-around of life, they were left out, and experienced boredom. It is natural for many teen-agers to experience similar periods of temporary boredom. Here are some practical steps that may help carry you and your youngster over the rough spots.

I. Get off the pedestal
Boredom is an inevitable, natural and mostly fleeting aspect of living. We all experience it, and it is important to remember that except in instances

of chronic depression concern about it need not be extreme.

When your kid is bored *don't patronize* him or her. *Don't say*, "When I was your age I didn't let myself get bored."

First of all, it's not true; you probably were bored more than you remember. Secondly, you will only turn your kid off. Don't act as if boredom is an affliction solely of the young. Try a bit of humility. Describe to your kid your own bouts with boredom.

If you convey to your child some of your own weaknesses, you will relieve some of his anxiety. He may even be encouraged to open up to you. The two of you may end up having a good laugh over the "trials and tribulations of life and growing up."

II. Don't be pushy. Listen

It is easy for parents to suggest things for bored kids to do: Call a friend; knit a sweater; do your homework; rake the lawn. But telling kids what to do is not going to help them. Kids know already what's available to them.

You might try just talking to your kid about things *other than his boredom*. Playing chess with Robert G. was helpful. In the course of our games, he was able to tell me much of the underlying causes of his boredom, and I was able to encourage him to explore some options of *his own choosing*. This is an important point.

A sullen teen-ager who rejects any advice or suggestions oftentimes will open up to talking. Try to find out if there is anything that might interest your child. It doesn't matter what it may be (as long as it is not destructive either to the child or somebody else). If your child comes up with an idea that seems outrageous to you, try to be encouraging. (Your daughter: "Maybe I could paint my room purple.") If you immediately tell her that she can't do that, you will be undermining the intimacy that you are trying to build up. *Go ahead*, let your daughter paint the room purple. When she grows tired of it, as she will, she can cure her next bout of boredom by painting it "shocking pink." (Note: Have *you* ever cured a bout of the "blues" by redecorating a room in your house?)

If you get to talking together, you might find it a good time to point out to your child how some of the more absurd messages of TV and other media actually tend to foster boredom by inflating expectations way out of proportion. Such a message, if it is perceived and understood, will go beyond just offering an insight into boredom; it will alert your child to look more critically at the barrage of messages we all are inundated with. It is a way of helping your child to become a better informed adult citizen in a free society.

III. Don't be defensive

Many teen-agers will attempt to blame their problems on others. Parents, being closest at hand, are easy targets for this kind of scatter-shot attack. *Don't retaliate* with counter-attacks of your own. This will only initiate a *blaming cycle*. If your child tries to throw blame on you, keep a clear head and a tight lip. Let your child know that you are not perfect, and that when he has simmered down, if he wants to pursue the matter you are willing to discuss any complaints that he may have. Let your teen-age children know that you are willing to drive them to certain functions, within reason; you will spend time with them, if they desire it; you will help them with homework, if they seriously seek help; you will listen to any other requests that they make, and you will try to offer guidance. But also let them know there is a limit beyond which you can do no more.

IV. Don't buy them off

Sometimes kids will take advantage of a parent's concern by trying to extort from them a present that they have been asking for. A very common ploy: "If you really loved me, you'd buy me a car, and then I wouldn't be bored."

If you fall for that one, you'll find that next time the ante goes up.

Don't be manipulated just because it hurts to see your loved one hurting a bit. Living through the blahs is a necessary part of growing up. By catering to every whim of adolescents, we simply reinforce their already unreal set of expectations. Part of growing up is learning to face obstacles and unpleasant states of feeling, and using one's own resources to alleviate the situation.

V. The rites of passage

Finally, remember, a temporary bout with boredom is part of the rite of passage for all teen-agers. Do not be overly concerned by occasional boredom. By all means, try to find out what is underlying any change in behavior of your teen-ager. If your child has been sociable and abruptly stops participating in activities which previously gave pleasure, it is important to understand what is going on. In the case of most teen-agers, nothing more is happening than that some changes are taking place within.

Adolescents moving from childhood to adulthood naturally will evolve new sets of interests, attitudes, and values which are more in keeping with a new sense of themselves. In dropping old habits and boycotting the usual repertoire of activities, for a time they may go through a form of human hibernation that hopefully will lead in new directions of a more adult and more deeply satisfying kind.

Problem #5

\\

"My Kid Is Doing Badly in School"

When young children leave the primary grades to enter Junior High School they are taking their first tentative steps into the world of adulthood. Not only are they moving into a higher stage of education, but they are moving into a world that is much less protective than they have ever known before. Instead of being taught by one teacher in the same familiar room for an entire year, they now find themselves in an environment that changes many times during the day. They have a homeroom teacher whom they may never actually see for a class. There are different teachers—men and women—whose classes they will attend for different subjects during the course of the day. There are long corridors to negotiate to get from one room to another; there are bells that announce the end of "periods"; there are many more children and adults mingling about than there ever were when they were in primary grades; some of the teachers have a difficult time just remembering the children's names.

Your child, at the age of 12 or 13, is being nudged out of the nest to make his or her first experimental flights. In real terms, this means that new educational and social demands are being made on your child, and you as a concerned parent naturally want your child to do well and to succeed. If your child has not been performing well academically up to this point, you naturally feel that *now* your child will begin to show his or her true brightness; and if your child has been performing well up to this point, you naturally assume that the spiral of success will continue onward and upward into ever more glorious heights of achievement.

Thus, when the day arrives that the phone rings and the Assistant Principal is on the line with the message that a child is performing badly academically, and also becoming a disruptive element in the classroom, the effect on the parent can be devastating. At first, you may find it almost impossible to believe. Sure, your little kid has been known to sass Mommy on one or two occasions, but a little stern talking to and a privilege taken away temporarily solved *that* particular problem. Sure, your kid's attention span has never been something to set new marks in the Guinness Book of Records. Sure, you had to spend a little extra time with your kid to help him or her learn the multiplication tables. Still, the idea of your kid being unable to do the academic work now being presented to him; or worse, that your kid is causing disruptions in the classroom, is *almost incredible*.

Your first reaction in such circumstances may very well be to get down to that school fast and give the Assistant Principal and your kid's teachers a good piece of your mind. *Nobody* has ever criticized your kid before. Well, yes, there was that *one* time when your child gave the next-door neighbor's child a "haircut" and the neighbor's child had to have his head shaved so that his hair could grow back evenly; and, yes, there was that other time when your child took another neighbor's bike apart to "fix" it, and didn't exactly know how to put it back together again. (Neither did you.) But—a *disruptive influence*! Never!

Parents are advised that it is, indeed, a good idea to visit the school when reports come in of bad academic or social performance. But they probably will do better to keep their tempers in check. Because *usually* reports from school of unsatisfactory performance are based on sound judgments, you can start by trusting that they reflect underlying problems that your child is having that need attention at home. When the evidence is presented by your child's teachers, usually the parents are obliged to bow to the truth that something is wrong.*

---

*If your teen-age child consistently performs poorly in school, the child should be evaluated by the school psychologist or by an outside consultant. Many kids whose academic performance is less than satisfactory (and, thus, oftentimes suffer secondarily from a low self-esteem leading to disciplinary problems) may have a learning disability in one or more areas. Problems connected with paying attention (attention deficit syndrome) may reflect learning problems in visual retention, auditory memory or even dyslexia (seeing world symbols in reverse), to name but a few. It should be emphasized that learning disabilities occur in people *with normal or even above normal intelligence*. Although many children outgrow or learn to compensate for learning problems, identification of the specific disabilities is extremely important since modification of school requirements and/

Once parents realize that there really is a performance problem on the part of their children, their next step often is to blame the child. "What's the matter with you?" is the most common exasperated question. "If you'd stop listening to the stereo, or watching TV, or spending so much time on the telephone you'd have more time for your homework and get better grades."

The perception that the child is wasting time on activities other than studying may very well be true, but this is only the tip of the iceberg. If your child all along has been assuring you that homework assignments have been done, while in point of fact they have not, then it follows that the child has been *lying*, too. It occurs to you that you may not have seen the child's last report card. Could your child have *withheld it from you and perhaps forged your signature*?! Where did your child learn such habits? Is the child hanging out with a *bad crowd*? What if your child is *hooked on drugs*?!

Other nightmares of a more long-range nature pop up. You find yourself wondering how your child will ever manage to get into college if he or she can't even pass a simple algebra course. (Parents tend to forget they may have had a bit of trouble with algebra themselves.) Will your child forever be helpless, unable to make a living? Will you have to support your child for the rest of your life?

And, finally, upon reflection, guilt may set in. "What did we do wrong, that our kid should be flunking three courses and be disrupting his classes?" Performance in school is perceived as the

or exposure to a wide variety of tutorial services can greatly enhance school performance. See also Problem #4 (Boredom), footnote page 83, regarding the extremely bright child.

first step toward success or failure in life. Generations of immigrants to this country have seen their children go on to positions of prominence and authority because of the educational opportunities afforded by a democratic society. Minority groups, too, have placed many of their hopes for advancement in the educational system. When their children perform badly, it is not just a matter of good or bad grades; it is for many parents the dashing of their fondest dreams. It would be difficult to say which parents suffer more: the Ivy League well-to-do successful professionals who have hopes to see their children follow in their own successful footsteps; or the grandchildren of immigrants, even the great grandchildren of slaves, who now have an opportunity to move into positions of financial security and power in the society that their family never knew. The configurations of our dreams may differ, but the pain is identical for all when the dreams are dashed.

Why Kids Do Poorly in School

As we have noted previously, teen-age children are going through a period of rapid change. New interests are crowding into their lives. To the Junior High School child, school is something that has been a part of his or her life for the past six, seven or eight years. But new interests, new sexual feelings, new *possibilities to explore* are presenting themselves to the teen-ager every day. For many teen-agers, at a certain point in their lives school tends to seem a lot less important than winning the esteem of the girl or boy at the next desk. If a certain amount of clowning around will catch that

other teen-ager's attention, a child may suddenly
find himself or herself in trouble with the teacher
for disruptive behavior in class. Homework is a daily
chore that often is boring and even at its best is
predictable. On the other hand, finding out where
the next party will be held provides excitement and
a sense of mystery.

Then there is a matter of paying attention in
class. Even the kids who are not clowning around
or thinking about parties are going through rapid
changes in maturity, which means that for the first
time in their lives they are beginning to form independent critical attitudes and opinions of their
own. Suddenly some of the teachers turn out to be
bores; another one has B.O.; a certain girl has "quite
a pair," and a certain boy is *gorgeous*. To the teen-
age child encountering a flood of new impressions
for the first time, *another kind of learning process*
is going on that is a lot more interesting than algebra, history, or English.

Many teen-age children go through periods when
they cannot handle with equal aplomb and ability
both the social and the academic learning processes
that they are experiencing in school. Some children
will manifest their confusion over the surfeit of new
sensations by temporarily doing poorly in their academic subjects. Very often the alert parent will detect this slackening off of school effort, and a bit of
friendly discussion and explaining will help a child
turn the corner and get back on the academic track
again. Sometimes it takes a bit longer, and talk
alone will not do the trick. A boy experiencing his
first sexual attractiveness to girls, or a girl experiencing her first serious "crush" on a boy can seem
to go "crazy" for awhile. But in most instances kids

themselves realize after awhile that, like it or not, there are serious tasks to perform in the adult world which they are now beginning to enter, and they tend to get back to serious work.

Although kids will be kids, there are certainly other instances in which poor performance in school is a sign of problems that go beyond mere distractibility and experimentation. It is one thing for a boy to show off and clown around to catch the attention of a girl he likes; it is quite another for him to compulsively clown about and disrupt a whole class because of a possible need for attention that is not coming from the home.

Parents who are going through problems in their own lives such as the trauma of a divorce, or who have suffered through the emotional drain of a long illness and death of a loved one, or who are deeply involved in career objectives, sometimes fail to provide the support and reassurance that teen-age children need. Children in such circumstances will often be the ones who in school make "funny faces" behind the teacher's back in an attempt to win the approval of their classmates.

In most instances, neglect of teen-age children is not conscious on the part of the parents; rather, it is due to the complexities of life that adults themselves are having difficulty dealing with. For example, if Mom and Dad seem to be totally preoccupied with a concern over Peter who at age 15 has already been arrested once for possession of "a controlled substance," as the police refer to marijuana and other drugs, 13-year-old Ann (who is confronting similar drug temptations) may start slacking off in school in an unconscious effort to get a bit of parental attention for herself. Her poor performance in school—*as it is in so many instances of children who are having school problems*—is nothing more than a cry for more attention.

Adult family bickering and an unhappy home environment can be contributing factors to a child's poor performance in school. When Jill, a 13-year-old eighth grader, complained about the constant fighting between her parents who had separated, then had gotten back together again twice within the past four years, she confessed to me that she lived in constant fear that her parents would divorce. To her, homework seemed like the most unimportant task in the world, in light of the heavy responsibility that she felt rested upon her: that of keeping her parents together.

In contrast to the mother and father who seem not to have enough time for their children are the parents who smother their teen-agers with appeals to excel in school. I am certainly in favor of children succeeding and winning all kinds of honors in school—*if they have the ability and if at any particular stage they have the inclination to excel.* It is a mistake, however, for parents to *push* their children too hard. Oftentimes, the results are negative rather than positive.

It always is a sad situation to encounter parents who are trying to enhance their own feelings of self-esteem through the accomplishments of their children. A child who is not able to measure up to the expectations of the parents can experience deep feelings of failure. Unfavorable comparisons with older siblings who have long since graduated with straight A's, or comparisons with the parent himself who may have excelled in the past, may cause the teen-ager simply to give up. In such instances, both the teen-ager and the parent experience deep disappointment. The parents may experience the teen-ager's poor performance as a direct slap in the face, while the child (more correctly) feels totally misunderstood. Such a child may feel as neglected as the child whose parents are too involved with their own problems to provide support and reassurance. What is happening in the instance of pushing children is that the over-emphasis on grades has resulted in a neglect of the child's *inner* feelings—his needs, true capabilities and aspirations. Feeling misunderstood, a teen-ager may give up or *deliberately fail*, again, in an effort to gain his parents' attention.

Sometimes teen-agers will show contempt and disdain for the educational system they are involved in because they have come to question the conventional wisdom: Success in School = Success in Life. Dad may have been Phi Beta Kappa at Harvard, and Mom may have been on the dean's list at Bryn Mawr, but to look at them now is to wonder, so what? After a hard day at the office Dad collapses in the evening in front of the TV, and Mom nips from the gin bottle she hides behind the V-8 juice in the refrigerator. All Dad can talk about is being "trapped" in the same boring job, and Mom is falling apart because of her family responsibilities. If this is the end result of success in school, the teen-ager—particularly the older teen-ager, who is being pressed to improve his grades to enter college, often concludes that he wants no part of it.

A generation ago, young teen-agers as a result of their disaffection over the nation's involvement in the war in Vietnam, tended to reject the success values of their parents altogether. Today, it seems to me, teen-age kids do not so much reject the success values of their parents, but they do tend to reject *the means to achieving* those values. *Glamor* is the new buzzword of success, and it would appear from almost any issue of PEOPLE magazine that one doesn't necessarily need an education to be glamorous and rich. Sylvester Stallone did not go to college.

Even in homes where there are no glaring signs of trouble the lives of the parents may lack appeal to today's teen-agers. Dad has his mid-week tennis game and week-end golf. Mom plays bridge on Thursday nights, and Mom and Dad together go out to dinner Saturday night. To today's teen-ager, this kind of life may seem too *boringly predictable*. There is a tendency on the part of the struggling teen-ager to feel: "What's the use of working hard in school? Is this all there is to life?"

Coping With the Teen-ager Who Is Doing Badly in School

As we noted in Problem #4 (Boredom), today's media plays a large part in the teen-ager's perception of what teen-life and young adult life are all about. In my opinion, most teen-agers do come to realize in time that life is not quite the glamorous beach party romp that the Pepsi ads make it out to be. Nevertheless, in the short run the teen-age child may rebel from what he perceives to be the dull routine of school which promotes the cut and dried professionalism of the adult world, and reject all notions that school can be a wonderfully enriching and life enhancing experience. Negotiating the rough waters between the time the young person passes from 13 to 18 can be a trying experience for parents who may often find themselves feeling that they need the wisdom of Solomon, the patience of Job, and the "luck of the Irish" to make it through. But I have found that as with the joke about old age—although it is unpleasant to be old and alone, the alternative is less attractive still—similarly with school: Kids may go through periods of hating it, but the alternative of pumping gasoline or busing dishes at "The Greasy Spoon" for the rest of one's life is not ultimately all that attractive either. In the case histories that follow we will take a look at how the parents of two different teen-agers changed their approach to their children with resulting helpful effects on school performance.

CASE STUDY I—LISA M.

The Complaint

At the very first meeting with Lisa M. and her mother, it was difficult for me to believe that Mrs. M. was describing her daughter. Here was this pretty, almost angelic 14-year-old girl, speaking in soft tones, and yet, she was being accused of not completing her homework assignments, of not even bothering to write them down, of missing the school bus at least two days each week, and also being truant on several occasions. Her grades were abysmally low. She didn't seem to care about anything connected with school at all.

The matter of missing the school bus was a particularly sore point with Mrs. M. because it meant that she would usually end up having to drive Lisa to school, with the result that she would arrive late at her job. The reasons for Lisa's missing the bus so often stemmed from the fact that every night she and her mother would argue about a suitable bedtime hour. The arguments were unsettling to both, but particularly to Lisa, who oftentimes would not be able to get to sleep until after midnight. The next morning, she would more than likely sleep through her alarm and her mother's wake-up call.

Additionally, Mrs. M. charged, Lisa bickered with her about doing chores around the house, and she exhibited a very lackadaisical attitude regarding an appropriate hour to arrive home after school. This, in Mrs. M.'s opinion, should be no later than 4:30. Although Lisa did, indeed, arrive home on most days by the appointed hour, there were a few lapses which Mrs. M. said were not acceptable.

Background

Mrs. M. had been married for 25 years, and only two years before, when Lisa was 12, after many years of bitter fighting, she and her husband had finally gotten a divorce. Within one year Mr. M. had remarried and had moved to California with his new young wife. Although he contributed some support for Lisa, Mr. M. wanted to make a new life, and felt it would be better if Lisa remained with her mother. Lisa's older sister was married and lived with her husband and small baby in Oregon. An older brother lived and worked in a nearby town.

After her separation Mrs. M. moved with Lisa into a small furnished apartment on the outskirts of town. Six months before she first came to my office she had met a man whom she hoped eventually to marry. At one private session I had with her Mrs. M. admitted that it would make her life "easier" if Lisa were living with her father. But, she said, Mr. M. was unwilling "to take Lisa off my hands."

"I need a little space to pick up the pieces of my life," Mrs. M. said.

Reaching Understanding

Although Mrs. M. wanted me to focus exclusively on Lisa's problems in school, it was obvious that we had to address ourselves to the bickering that was going on between mother and daughter in the home.

Meeting with the two of them together, we discussed Mrs. M.'s need at the present time for "order and clarity" in her life. The kind of behavior she was demanding from Lisa was that of a mature "roommate" who would make no demands and, even more than that, take on the lion's share of cleaning and keeping the house in order. To Mrs. M., it seemed as if she couldn't function if Lisa wasn't in bed promptly every night by 10:30, and home from school every day by 4:30. She had had enough "chaos" in her life as a result of the divorce from Mr. M. She was terrified, she admitted, of losing her new boyfriend.

Once these admissions had come from Mrs. M. the confessional floodgates opened for Lisa, too. Not wanted by her father, missing her older brother and sister, and sensing full well her mother's ambivalence toward her very presence in the house, Lisa was experiencing profound feelings of insecurity and lowered self-esteem. With nowhere to go, and trapped into the regimentation demanded of her by her troubled and harrassed mother, Lisa was feeling the uselessness of struggle, and *didn't care*. As a consequence, she simply *didn't bother* to take down her homework assignments. It no longer seemed to matter to her whether she did well in school, or not.

Creative Synthesis

With everyone's cards on the table, it was obvious that both Lisa and her mother were tired of fighting. They were looking for a solution, but couldn't seem to find a way out of their circle of conflict.

I picked out what seemed to me to be the two most glaring problems relating to Lisa's difficulties in school. The first step had to come from Mrs. M. After all, Lisa was the 14-year-old in the equation. Mrs. M. needed immediately to stop arguing with Lisa over her bedtime hour, and let Lisa determine for herself when she wanted to go to bed. (Lisa suggested that "around ten" made a lot of sense). If they stopped bickering about the bedtime hour, I said, maybe Lisa would get to sleep earlier, and be able to get up in time to catch the school bus.

It was made clear to Lisa, however, that Mrs. M. would *cease immediately* driving Lisa to school. If Lisa missed the bus, that was her responsibility, not her mother's. This arrangement seemed to be agreeable to both mother and daughter.

Finally, I addressed the need of *both* mother and daughter for privacy and time to spend with their own peer groups. Mrs. M. definitely needed time to spend alone with her boyfriend, and Lisa needed more freedom to work out her relationships with her school chums. Lisa, I pointed out to her mother, no longer had a sister and brother in the house, and her father was making a new life in California. She should be allowed to spend more time with friends after school, and should be allowed to bring friends home, or go to a friend's house, providing she made arrangements ahead of time.

Once again, both mother and daughter agreed that these suggestions made sense, and they could live with them.

The end result was that after just four weeks and four more family sessions, Lisa and her mother were on their way to a much-improved home environment that immediately was reflected in Lisa's improved attitude and performance in school.

At our last meeting Lisa happily reported that she had made two new school friends, and in recent tests she had "felt good about knowing the answers" and was hoping that with continued effort she would be able to bring her average up to a B. Her mother confirmed that Lisa had missed the school bus only once in the past four weeks, and she was getting her homework written down and it was being done every day.

Generally, both mother and daughter reported, Lisa was asleep by 10:15. Sometimes she was actually in bed by 9:30. Lisa seemed like a different girl. She even mentioned the fact that she wanted her mother to have more time with "Ed" (the boyfriend).

CASE STUDY II—DAVID R.

The Complaint

David was 14 and a ninth grader when he was referred to me by the school guidance counselor because of mediocre school performance. Described by his father as "a nice boy," David was repeating ninth grade because he had not done well the first year, and his parents had felt he needed the additional time to "mature."

David's teachers were somewhat less sympathetic and forgiving than his parents as they assessed him as unmotivated, inattentive, a day dreamer, and somewhat surly and angry. He was just barely making a C-minus average, despite the fact that all aptitude tests showed him capable of doing B-plus, or even A work.

Speaking in a professional but loving manner, Mr. R. considered his son's primary problem to be one of low self-confidence. "David is on the passive side, but always willing to help around the house," Mr. R. reported in a somewhat affectionate manner.

In subsequent sessions, it quickly became apparent that although David may have been passive around his father, there was nothing passive about his feelings toward both of his parents, though this only came out when he was apart from them. "My mother yells at me all the time, and my father lectures—oh, my God, lectures, lectures, lectures," David said.

When I asked him to be more specific, David complained that failure to complete a homework assignment, or even something as innocuous as forgetting to close the refrigerator door, would be grounds for an angry explosive outburst from his mother and a good half-hour of "discussion" (mostly one-way) from Mr. R.

Unlike the parents of most of his friends, Mr. R. demanded that David use "proper speech" (i.e., no colloquialisms or slang words), and that he dress in impeccably neat attire. In a desire to help his children earn higher grades, Mr. R. was having David and his older brother Philip and his younger sister Angela privately tutored (even though Philip was earning an A average in 11th grade, and Angela was getting a B-plus average in 6th grade).

David felt as though he could never fight back against his father. He conceded that it was easier to "keep quiet" around both his mother and father, whom he couldn't win against anyway, and let off steam occasionally in the company of his friends. In exchange for "keeping quiet" around his father, and not confronting him with his real feelings, he admitted that he got back some advantages in return. Mr. R. really did look upon David as "a nice boy," and, in fact, treated him as his favorite. David was able to use his good image with Dad as leverage for gaining some of the material things and privileges that he wanted.

Background

One couldn't help but be impressed by Mr. R. At the age of 64, he had accomplished feats that ranked him well above those of most men. Handsome, tall and straight, graying at the temples, he seemed like a modern Renaissance man, excelling at most anything he attempted to do. A club level tennis champion, an accomplished pianist, a skillful cabinet maker, he was also considered a "real estate genius" by all who knew him in business. He had begun by buying property of moderate value and, after fixing it up, selling it at a handsome profit. He now presided over a prestigious realty company with diversified holdings and a staff of 25 people.

Mr. and Mrs. R. made a strikingly handsome couple. Mrs. R., still a beauty at 46, was born in Austria, and with her European background tended to defer to her husband's strong personality. Talking to her, I could not help but feel that because she, very much like David, could not stand up to her husband in a direct confrontation, she tended to be "passive" in his presence. However, she was fiery underneath and the fire would come out particularly when David's lapses (like leaving the refrigerator door open) caused an upset in the family routine.

Interestingly, despite David's poor performance in school, both Mr. and Mrs. R. saw him being more like Mr. R. than their older son Philip. Though prone to somber moods and below potential grades, David often demonstrated a charismatic charm (used to good effect on his father) that reminded both parents of the younger Mr. R. When motivated, David showed a great aptitude for tennis and, in the winter months, ice hockey. He was also blessed with a charming somewhat self-effacing sense of humor. Despite his poor grades, he excelled in sciences, surprising everyone on occasion by bringing home A's on exams and laboratory projects.

Reaching Understanding

What became clearly apparent very early in our meetings together was the distinction between David's tendency to avoid confrontations with his father and the opposite almost disrespectful and openly provocative approach of both his older brother and younger sister toward Mr. R. Both Philip and Angela would stand up to their father and, as a result, paid a price of punishment ranging from prohibitions against going out on week-ends to endless lecturing on the evils of disobedience.

Although David escaped the fate of his brother and sister, on the inside he was boiling with anger. In exchange for the pay-off of his father's good opinion of him, David actually was paying a greater price than his brother and sister. He was exhibiting symptoms of mild depression which gave indication of becoming worse, and it was being reflected in a downward spiral of increasingly bad grades in school.

It was time to alert Mr. R. to what was really going on in the relationship that had grown up and become established between himself and David. At a family meeting, I laid the facts out clearly for everyone to take a look at. By being passive to the personality and demands of Mr. R., David was holding in his own true feelings; he was, in short, sacrificing his guts to his father's lofty self-image. David had had it impressed upon him for so long about what a "wonderful" success his father was, he simply could not bring himself to express his own true feelings in the presence of his father. Only by achieving well below Mr. R.'s fondest expectations could David vent his real anger and thus defeat his father. Failing, or performing below average, was David's way of asserting his own independence through surreptitious punishment of Mr. R.

Things began to fall into place for David as soon as he realized that there were acceptable alternatives to passivity in the home. Mr. R., once he was able to see what was going on with David, actually encouraged his son to speak his real feelings. We had some "wild" sessions when David first began to externalize his feelings toward his parents.

As a result of his being able for the first time to express himself, and to speak up when he had grievances of his own, to stand on his own two legs and fight back when he felt that unjust demands were being made on him, David's self-confidence (which Mr. R. had originally pointed to correctly as the key to David's progress) actually began to grow by leaps and bounds. Within three months we all witnessed a dramatic transformation within David. His grades began to improve, and soon he was up to a B-plus average. He won first prize in the spring science fair, and he was playing Number Three on the school tennis team. As his confidence continued to develop and as his success in school activities also grew, David's former depression began to fade. David's progress also had a good effect on the whole family. Mr. R., having been "chastened" somewhat by the developing events of life, tended to lecture less, and listen more. David admitted to me at our last session together that "the old man is all right," which for a teen-ager oftentimes can be highest praise.

Practical Steps

The cases of Lisa M. and David R. are quite different. Lisa, whose mother was overwhelmed by personal problems of her own, felt unwanted, with the result that school seemed like a secondary factor in her life. In the case of David, great expectations were held out for him by a strong-minded parent whom David felt powerless to stand up against. Whereas Lisa reacted by "giving up," David took the tack of "punishing" his father by performing below his potential.

I. Look for the underlying causes of your child's poor school performance

Despite the differences between Lisa M. and David R., both children did a turn-about after their parents were able to make adjustments in the way they related to them. Parents with concerns about the school performance of their children will be well advised to *look for the underlying causes* of their children's problems, rather than scold or punish or give up on them as a lost cause.

If a child who is doing poorly in school is tested and found not to have learning disability, perhaps he or she is disturbed over friction that is occurring between the parents in a household. If so, perhaps family counselling for the *parents* is indicated.

Does your child feel *excluded from the social scene* of his peers? Is he asserting himself negatively in school as a response to *too much parental dominance in the home*? Has he or she *suffered the loss of a close friend or relative*, either as a result of a death or a move away to another city? Is there something in your child's life that is causing him or her to be depressed?

The concerned parent should ask himself the above questions in an attempt to uncover any underlying problems.

II. What are your kid's real capabilities?

One of the worst things a parent can do is to demand more of a child than he or she is capable of. Not all kids are meant to be scientists, doctors, or lawyers. By making unreasonably high demands, parents will only succeed in creating some form of resistance in their kids, whether it be overt rebellion (e.g., insubordination), covert sabotage (e.g. the child says he is completing homework assignments when he isn't), or excessive compliance. The latter response may actually portend more serious adjustment problems in the future, since overly compliant behavior sometimes is related to an inability to achieve emotional independence from the parents.

Although parents should not lower their standards *automatically* when their teen-ager is experiencing difficulty, nevertheless, a realistic set of expectations based on a close observation of the child, plus consultations with school authorities, and possible testing, oftentimes can put matters in better perspective.

Not all kids are intellectually equipped to go to college. If your child has trouble passing history, English, or math, it may very well be that he or she has other strengths. Perhaps your child has artistic or musical talents; perhaps your child is handy with tools; perhaps your child's talents are exclusively in the area of *athletics*. Encourage your child's strengths, while supporting your child to whatever extent necessary in his or her weaker areas. The most important thing for you to realize is that *your teen-ager ultimately should be motivated by something that fulfills his or her inner needs for accomplishment.*

III. Be a partner, not an adversary

It is natural for teen-agers to revolt. After all, many of today's so-called yuppies were hippies in the 1960's. If your child is of a rebellious nature and seems always to be "going against the stream," whether at home or at school, my advice is *don't come down on the child too hard.*

Rebellious behavior today is conventional behavior tomorrow. If your kid's behavior seems (to you) somewhat outlandish, whether it be an interest in motorcycles, or rock music, or a "punk" hairstyle (instead of the traditional Little League baseball, Pop Warner football, or tennis at the club), try not to be too disapproving. True, your kid probably won't want to share his interests with you. ("Aw, Dad, you won't enjoy 'The Grateful Dead.' ") Still, there are ways that you can let your teen-age children know that *you do not reject them because of their lifestyle choices.* Maybe your kid will ask you to drive him to a motorcycle meet. Maybe you can interest your kid in a subscription to a music scene periodical. (Not a bad way of encouraging him to read, incidentally.) At the very least, try to stay close to what your children are interested in. Let them know that even though you don't want to go to the rock concert with them, you know how important contemporary music is to kids today. (Remember Do-wop, Do-wop of 25 years ago?) By avoiding the tendency to say "no" to your children's every outlandish desire, in time they will come to appreciate how lucky they have been to have had such understanding parents.

Listen to your kids. It's entirely possible that your kids can teach you something about life that you don't know. We can all benefit through growth, and sometimes the insights of children are the truest insights of all.

IV. The positive bribe

Bribery is something we have learned to think of as wrong. But all bribes are not the same as all other bribes. When you make an agreement with your teen-age kid to buy him or her a new 10-speed bike or a tapedeck for the car in exchange for improvement in grade point average, you are following the principle that psychologists call *operant conditioning*. A layman might prefer to call it an incentive. A moralist might tend to call it a bribe.

Whatever you want to call it, an incentive will influence a person's behavior only if it is *truly* an incentive—something that the person to whom it is offered really values. Just because *you* place a high value on tickets to a Broadway musical, it doesn't automatically follow that your child does, too. Let your child suggest an appropriate reward, and if you decide that it is within the limits of a reasonable demand, agree to it.

Eventually, when your child begins to achieve good grades on a regular basis, he will begin to find that success itself is its own reward: the accolade of teachers, parents, his peers. His own self-respect and pride are the most satisfying rewards of all.

A word of caution: Don't set a standard of performance for your teen-ager that the child can't meet, for example, demanding straight A's during the very next term. If a child knows that he cannot win the reward, he will not try to earn it; rather, he may resent the attempt to manipulate him, and, nursing his resentment, give up altogether.

Finally, don't expect your kid to continue to improve indefinitely with only one reward. If your kid is able to raise his grades by 10 percent, for example, from D to C, set the next standard a little higher, and offer another reward after he attains the first goal. (Remember, always bear in mind the real limits and capabilities of your child.)

V. Taking time off

Some kids may need to step outside the mainstream of the educational process and work for awhile. A job oftentimes will take pressure off until the teen-ager better understands himself or herself, or determines a new set of priorities.

Working can provide a teen-ager with a new perspective on life. A teen-ager who works for awhile very often will come to realize on his own that unskilled work (the kind he is most likely to be able to get without a high school eduction) isn't all that great, after all. In such instances, the teen-ager may be happy to return to school, and in such circumstances *frequently will exhibit new levels of high performance upon returning.*

I am certainly not advocating that kids should drop out of school just because the going may get rough from time to time. What I am saying is that sometimes a temporary hiatus from the rigors of pressures at home and at school may be beneficial, *if all other avenues have been tried.* Parents, naturally, fear that when a child quits school to work he or she will never return to academia again. But in many cases, I have found, the child is usually ready to return for the next academic year. In any event, after a certain age, a parent cannot *force* a teen-ager to go to school. In instances where a teenager determines that he or she will not go back to school, a parent can be most helpful in guiding the youngster into the kind of job that will best suit his or her emotional and financial needs.

Problem #6

//

"My Kid and I Can't Talk to Each Other"

How many times have you tried to give your teen-age son or daughter a small piece of advice only to be interrupted in midsentence by an exasperated, "I *kno-o-o-w!*"

The fact is, *you* know that your child probably does *not* know. Still, there is no convincing him or her of that. Their use of the words, "I know," means: Forget it; I'm not listening; don't talk about it anymore; you don't know anything; leave me alone.

It would be bad enough if it just ended with that, but as often as not this attitude teen-agers have of not wanting parental interference carries over into a more generalized basic behavior pattern of cutting off all but the most essential and rudimentary communication with their parents. That sweet little girl or that cute little guy who used to give a cheery, "Hi, Mom!" each time he or she popped into a room you were in, no matter how many times within the course of any five-minute period, now suddenly has turned into a sullen lout who treats you like an intruder, and communicates largely by means of grunts and scowls, if not outright groans.

The first reaction of a parent who is beginning to experience a lack of conversational give-and-take with their teen-age child is oftentimes one of hurt. Why, all of a sudden, does your kid seem to dislike you so much? What have you done to deserve such surly treatment? *You* really haven't changed all that much. What is it that has changed your kid?

In addition to being hurt, parents *worry* about the child who suddenly clams up and has nothing to say. Is it possible your kid is growing up to be a moody social misfit? Such fears are usually dispelled when the parent catches a glimpse of the child in the presence of his or her peer group. (Usually, you catch a glimpse of how your kid is doing with other kids only from a distance, possibly by looking surreptitiously through a window.) Glimpsed from afar, there's your kid, exuding charm, and engaged in animated conversation with his friends. No, your child is not a social misfit; it's just that he simply won't talk to *you*, his parent.

And what about reports from other adults who know your child? Oftentimes, speaking of that child of yours who grunts and mumbles and gives you surly looks around the house, teachers and neighbors will go out of their way to tell you how courteous he is, how polite and generally well-mannered.

As pleased and relieved as you may be to see that your child functions well with his peers and to learn that other adults think highly of him, at a certain point the hurt and concern that you have been feeling may begin to turn into anger.

"That little wimp!" one mother exclaimed to me one day in my office. "I brought him into this world. I changed his dirty diapers. I suffered through the 'terrible twos' and all the other 'terrible traumas', and tried to be a good parent, and what do I get in return? *Nothing!* Not even a 'good morning' at the breakfast table."

Parents who become angry or feel bewildered in this way may have moments when they simply feel like "giving up" on their child, adopting the attitude, "If my child can't act like a civilized person to me, I'm not going to act civilized toward him." Such an attitude is understandable, but, needless to say, only tends to make a tense situation worse.

Surprisingly, parents often discover that when, in exasperation, they blow up at a teen-ager, as likely as not the child is completely bewildered by the outburst. One father told how after he had exploded in anger at his daughter, she went to his wife, and complained, "What's the matter with Dad, Mom? I think he needs a vacation."

Communication (or lack of it) consists of more than just words, too. If a child is generally uncommunicative, that means he or she is not volunteering very much to help out around the house. The basic attitude seems to be one of deliberate non-cooperation.

How can any adult maintain sanity living in a house with such a moody, unpredictable creature as an uncommunicative teen-ager? You feel you are making every effort, and getting nothing in return. Worse, your child may actually manage to challenge your own perception of yourself. Instead of being appreciated for the reasonable, intelligent, perceptive, and controlled adult that you really are, you suddenly find yourself being treated like an idiot, a fool, or a jackass. Your child won't listen to anything you have to say, and doesn't volunteer to say anything to you. There is a lot of silence in the house, with anger boiling on the inside.

Most importantly, there are *some matters* that parents simply *must discuss* with their children if they are to carry out their parental guidance responsibilities. But when every matter brought up for discussion, no matter how diplomatically initiated, is resented and resisted, the end result can be exhausting and frustrating. Parents cannot help but wonder how they got themselves into this non-communication bind in the first place, and if a time will ever arrive when members of the family can go back to acting like civilized people again.

Why Teen-agers and Their Parents Don't Communicate

If ever there was a Catch-22 situation, it applies to the matter of communication between the teenage child and his parents. At a time in the teenager's life when he is still almost totally reliant on his parents for the basics of his very life—food, clothing, shelter, education, emotional support—at the same time he has never struggled harder to be completely on his own.

The inevitable contradiction is likely to lead to conflict.

Take, for example, the simple matter of your teen-ager's borrowing the family car. In a typical scenario, it's Friday night, and your son asks to borrow your car. Okay, so the answer is, "Yes."

The son gets dressed up—meaning he puts on a clean pair of jeans and T-shirt (that Mom washed for him)—calls a couple of friends (using the family telephone), and after wolfing down his supper (which his mother prepared for him), he is ready to go. As you hand over the keys you say, "Don't forget, no beer in the car. Drive carefully. Be home by one o'clock."

What does your teen-ager reply? "I *know*, Dad."

Your son takes the keys, mumbling thanks, and gets into the car. You cringe as he "burns rubber" going out the driveway. For the rest of the evening you try to occupy your mind with a variety of interests of your own—reading, television, conversation, whatever—but always in the back of your mind is that nagging worry about the time when the car—and your son—will be safely home again.

Meanwhile, your kid is king for the night as he cruises around town with his buddies, impressing the local girls, stopping in at the bowling alley for a Coke, pushing the accelerator to the floor on a lonely stretch of highway on the edge of town.

At one o'clock sharp, your teen-ager pulls the car into the driveway (assuming the best). As the motor is turned off, the feeling that comes over your teen-ager is a little like the emotion that Cinderella must have felt when at the stroke of midnight her coach was turned into a pumpkin and her horses into mice. Home is *reality* again. The car that provided your son with a few hours of feeling like a king isn't *his* car; it's *Dad's* car. Your son isn't free at all. He is *dependent* on his parents for granting him a few hours of feeling independent. How grateful can he be when what he wants more than anything else at this stage of his life is to be *free*? Is it any wonder that at breakfast the next morning he isn't bubbling over with cute stories about what a great time he and his buddies had last night in your car? If he can't have a car of his own, the thing that *is* his own is the experience of a few hours apart from those who, in one sense, he can only see as his "captors," and he will zealously guard the precious secrecy of those few free moments and keep them to himself.

Parents have a difficult time understanding this need for privacy and secretiveness on the part of teen-agers. What is most annoying is that even when parents do their kids a favor—like lending them the family car—the kids are unable to respond with much gratitude or appreciation.

"You don't appreciate all the things we do for you," is a common complaint of parents to their teen-age children.

But, as we have just seen, it is the nature of teen-agers to *resent* the very things they depend on their parents to do for them. How can they be expected to display their appreciation?

Then there is the matter of providing *parental guidance* to teen-age children. If teen-agers resent even the privileges and support that parents provide to them, imagine how they feel when constraints are imposed on them in an effort to guide and control them. Teen-agers think they know everything; and even if they don't know, they don't want to be reminded that they don't. It is a period in their life when *they want to find out for themselves*. For 13 years or so everything has been done for them. Now the time has arrived when they will test their mettle. Unfortunately, their mettle often exceeds their wisdom, and parents wouldn't be doing their job if they didn't step in sometimes, and impose restrictions.

Sure, your daughter "knows" that you want her in by such-and-such a curfew hour; your son "knows" that he should not show off and drive the family car too fast; they both "know" that they are not supposed to hang out with a certain crowd, that they should do their homework before going out, that there are certain chores to do around the house.

Yet, despite their claim that they "know" these things, there is evidence to prove the contrary. There is a dent in the front fender of the family car from the last time they were allowed to take it out. They are doing poorly in school. The garbage is overflowing onto the floor, and the dishes have not been done.

Teen-agers do not know as much as they think they do, and, unquestionably, in most instances they do not know as much as you do. But when you find it necessary to guide or control them in instances where you know they are wrong, or over their heads, they have a difficult time accepting your discipline.

This conflict between what you know about your teen-agers and what is best for them and what they think they know about themselves is one of the root causes of what is sometimes referred to as "the generation gap."

Take, for example, one instance that was brought to my attention of a 16-year-old daughter who announced to her parents one weekend that she was going *sky-diving* with her boyfriend. This girl's parents were reasonably liberal-minded and understood the spirited nature of their daughter, but nevertheless, they had some serious reservations about allowing her to go off with a boy they hardly knew, to a sky-diving airfield that even their daughter didn't know the location of, to jump out of an airplane.

When they gently questioned their daughter about some of the details, she became furious, storming around the house, and complaining that her parents didn't understand her, didn't allow her any "civil rights," informing them, finally, that whether her parents wanted her to go sky-diving or not, she was going to go, whether today or some other day, and there was absolutely nothing they could do about it.

At this point, though the parents were quite alarmed, they maintained a common-sense attitude, and telephoned the parents of the boyfriend. Their phone call came during the midst of a similar scene at the boyfriend's house, since the boy's parents, too, had just learned of their son's plans a few minutes before.

The boy was as adamant as the girl about going sky-diving, but since, it turned out, there was the small matter of a $150 fee for sky-diving, which neither the boy nor the girl had, plus the need to borrow Dad's car to get to the airfield, the expedition was nipped in the bud right there. (A postscript to the story is that by the time this spirited young lady had raised the $150 sky-diving fee by doing babysitting jobs, she had long since lost interest in the boyfriend, and at the same time her interest in jumping out of an airplane.)

In this example, we have a situation where the

parents felt obliged to block an activity of their teen-ager that they had good reason to feel was misguided. Sky-diving may very well be a legitimate activity, even for teen-agers, but, at the very least, it is not something that should be undertaken casually, without parental supervision and some sobering discussion.

Although parents of teen-agers clearly have a responsibility to step in and guide the activities of their children, at the same time it is understandable why teen-agers tend to resent what they consider as interference in their young lives. What often happens in such a situation is that the child tends to see the parent as "the bad guy," and resists guidance. Thus, the parent is forced into a position of actually *becoming* "the bad guy" in order to exercise an influence. This leads to more resistance by the child and, in turn, to further "interference" by the parents in a spiralling syndrome sometimes referred to by psychologists as a "feedback loop." The result is a mutual defensiveness on both sides as a consequence of an intense shared resentment that ultimately prevents either the parents or the teen-age child from seeing the other's point of view. Unable to appreciate each other's point of view, the open exchange of ideas inevitably breaks down.

Ironically, when this kind of breakdown occurs, *both* sides experience feelings of abandonment. The parents will state that their child is "ungrateful and uncaring." The teen-ager will assert, "They don't care about me."

Contributing to the lack of communication between teenagers and their parents is the certain assumption on the part of most teen-agers that their parents will never be able to understand them or their interests, or what they are going through. They know intellectually that their parents, too, must have been teen-agers once, but it is impossible for them to believe that the teen-age problems faced by their parents have any relevance to the problems that they face now. Certainly the "generation gap" is not narrowed by statements from the parents to the effect, "When I was your age, I—" When used by the parents to buttress an argument, such statements only serve to prove to adolescents that their parents are completely out of touch with present-day reality.

And sometimes the kids can be right. Times *have* changed, and trying to bring up kids today the way kids were brought up 25 years ago just doesn't work. Children who are trying to find out who they are, how they measure up in life, what they can do on their own, are more likely to listen and pay attention to the opinions and behavior of their peer group than they are to a lot of out-of-touch advice from Mom and Dad.

Consider, for example, the matter of the educational and career interests exhibited by the majority of teen-agers today. In the 1960's, college kids (when they weren't burning their bras or draft cards) tended to aim toward liberal arts college courses. Today, the preferred choice of bright high school graduates (the offspring of that earlier generation) is a career in business or computer science.* Teaching, which was a popular choice for teen-agers 25 years ago, today is not even considered by many children. Hospitals once flooded with

*N.Y. *Times*, March 25, 1984. *N.Y. Times*, July 25, 1984.

applications for student nurse training, now find it difficult to recruit enough nurses to handle their needs. Whatever opinion one may have about these matters, one cannot deny that times have changed. And parents often seem to be the last to know.

Faced with a series of parental responses to their problems that seem hopelessly out of touch with present-day reality and peer-pressure demands, teen-age kids tend to "turn off and tune out" guidance and advice from parents.

There is another aspect, too, to the tendency of teen-agers to withdraw from verbal communication with their parents. The teen-age years are a time when youngsters are prone to deep introspection which oftentimes takes on the appearance of brooding.

Teen-age kids *don't know themselves*. At the same time, they feel the need to find out who they are. The pressure on them to make adult decisions comes at them from every direction: from their parents, from school authorities, from their peers, from advertising messages. They feel awkward, and oftentimes "just plain dumb" and unready. They are trying to find out how they measure up to the opposite sex, how they get along with members of their own sex, how they are *different* and individual, and how they are the same. These are matters that concern them a great deal of the time.

"What will I do, and what will I become," are fundamental questions that loom over teen-agers, and often cause them to withdraw not only from parents, but even temporarily from each other. And the answers are rarely immediately forthcoming. The plain fact is that most kids, for a time at least, do not know themselves. They don't know how to behave in social situations. (Neither do some adults.) If they look an adult in the eye, shake hands, will that adult be able to see into their innermost souls? Looking away and remaining silent may be a way of avoiding being laughed at, or counselled, or judged as "weird."

You may not remember, but *you* were this way once yourself. The process by which you grew up involved learning how to *cover up* many of your own doubts and fears about yourself and your relationship to life. You spent many years building up a defensive shield. Even your vaunted "openness" with other people may be a way of holding them off from your innermost thoughts. Perhaps you have become adept at ingratiating yourself with people. You can charm them, intimidate them, manipulate them, whatever. But the development of all these techniques took time, and once there was a time when you did not have them perfected.

A teen-ager often wonders if he or she will ever be able to develop the social skills of the adults they see about them. And because they are not sure, because they are afraid, in fact, are intimidated, they may very well withdraw into a shell of silence. How much easier it would be if they could only trust you and share with you their fears! But even if they did feel they could trust you, they might not be able to speak up. Simply because they are so conflicted and confused they don't even know what questions to ask. The unfortunate part is that parents oftentimes cannot help but experience this period of temporary immobilization on the part of their teen-agers as rejection, or purposeful shunning of them.

Coping with the
Uncommunicative Teen-ager

A certain amount of awkwardness and inability to communicate is inevitable on the part of youngsters during their teen-age years. Until such time as your teen-ager crosses over into adulthood and begins to feel comfortable in communicating with you again, there are some steps you can take that may help speed its arrival. Before we take a look at some practical suggestions, let's examine a typical case history from my files.

CASE STUDY—DARRELL B.

The Complaint

At first glance, Darrell B. gave the impression of being the "all-American boy." At 16 years of age he was close to six feet tall, with a good pair of football shoulders, and a nice smile. A note from his father that preceded the family's first visit to my office, however, gave a different impression. According to Mr. B.'s note, Darrell, with a C-minus average, was not doing well in school. His teachers had reported home that Darrell was unmotivated in his studies, inattentive and easily distracted in class, and, even more disturbing, on several occasions had been disrespectful.

Both Mr. and Mrs. B. were reasonably enlightened parents, and immediately recognized that "something" was going on with their son that was causing problems for him. One of the first things that they had done, Mrs. B. told me at our first meeting, was to sit down informally around the kitchen table and try to find out from Darrell what, if anything, was wrong. It was Darrell's negative reaction to that particular meeting and a general negative attitude during weeks that followed that more than anything else made his parents decide that Darrell needed professional help.

Mrs. B. spoke right up: "I'm not at all sure what Darrell is thinking about most of the time. He used to be such an open boy. We used to discuss everything. Now it's impossible to even have a normal conversation with him without his becoming angry."

Darrell's father jumped in. "I don't understand him. He's a bright boy, good-looking. We're behind him 100 per cent. He knows that. Still, it's impossible to get anything out of him."

To which Darrell replied: "Things are kind of confused right now. I'm having a little trouble sorting things out, I guess."

Background

Darrell came from a family that might be described as "enlightened." His father was a tenured English professor at a nearby university, with a reputation on campus for being something of a spokesman for students' rights. His mother was a psychiatric social worker, working with a state agency on adult alcoholic problems.

A younger brother, Larry, was 14, and seemed to have no problems at school. His average was A-minus, and like Darrell, he had an "all-American" look about him.

There were differences between Mr. and Mrs. B.

Mr. B. was the son of working-class parents, and had risen to his present position in life by "hard work and trying to be the best that I could." Like many self-made men, he believed that the secret to success was self-discipline. Although he tried to be scrupulously fair, he was also a stern "go-by-the-book" disciplinarian.

Talking with the family at one of our sessions, Mr. B. let it be known that one of the greatest fears in his life was that the next generation (his children) would slip back into blue-collar working-class circumstances. "I don't want to see the old adage, 'from shirtsleeve to shirtsleeve in two generations' come to be a reality in *this* family," he said.

Mrs. B. on the other hand, was much more relaxed than her husband. Having come from a long line of professional people, including a grandmother who had been a prominent women's rights suffragette advocate, she felt the family's social position to be more secure. As a professional psychiatric social worker, her inclination was to be more sympathetic toward her son, and to seek ways of understanding Darrell's inner world of thoughts and feelings.

Reaching Understanding

Although there was very little communicating between Darrell and his parents, he was not reticent to talk to me. Once a kid realizes that I am not an instrument of his parents and out to control him, he usually opens up. The problem in Darrell's case, however, was that he had no idea as to why he felt closed off.

"I'm trying to figure things out," Darrell confided. "But I don't know where I stand. I don't know what people think of me, whether they think I'm a nerd, or cool, or what. I don't know myself." Then he looked at me intently. "What do you think?"

I certainly did not think that he was a nerd. I suggested that it might help if we got an insight into how he felt about his family. From that point on, we began to make progress.

His mother and father, Darrell stated, were "really behind me all the way." Then he added, "Maybe too much." Mr. B., pushing to see that Darrell developed into an "achiever" like himself, was always stepping in to help him. If Darrell had to fill out a form for school, his father was there to make sure that he did it right. His father, Darrell told me, would spend every Saturday morning with him drilling him in tennis. "He thinks I like it, but I'm getting sick of it," Darrell said. "I'd rather be jammin' with the guys."

Darrell complained that his father expected him to go to tennis camp the following summer, whereas what he wanted to do was to get a job at a neighborhood gas station where a lot of his friends hung out, and make some money for an expensive electric guitar and sound system.

"Why don't you tell him what you want to do?" I asked Darrell.

"He doesn't listen to me!" Darrell exploded. "Well, okay, he hears the words, but he doesn't listen to what it *means* to me."

This, I thought, was a pretty clear exposition of the problem, coming as it did from a kid who supposedly was having troubles communicating.

Darrell's mother, on the other hand, encouraged Darrell to do what he wanted to do on his own, but wanted to know all the time *why* he was doing it. "She's always asking me all these questions," he said. "Sometimes I wish she'd leave me alone. I feel like telling her sometimes to just *shut up*."

What was clear from Darrell's comments was that there was no lack of effort on the part of his parents to do what was right to help him, but pitifully little awareness of the negative impact their efforts and insights were having on him.

Creative Synthesis

Sometimes it's harder to convince extremely intelligent people that they are making mistakes than it is to convince people who are not on as high an intellectual level. Both Mr. and Mrs. B. were convinced that their opinions about raising their teenage sons were sound.

The problems that Darrell was experiencing were largely of his own making, they felt.

"If only he would apply himself in school," Mrs. B. said.

"And take some responsiblity around the house," Mr. B. added.

"If he would spend more time with us, and less time brooding, or playing that music he listens to."

"If only he would understand how much we care about him, and realize what a terrific kid we think he is."

Usually I prefer the subtle approach, but sometimes I feel it's necessary to wield a sledge-hammer. "But do you realize how angry Darrell is with you, Mr. and Mrs. B.?" I asked.

"Well, we're angry with him, too!" Mrs. B. shot back.

"Probably that's why the two sides are not communicating," I replied.

This was a critical exchange. Both sides admitted that they were angry with the other, but neither side was willing to budge. I directed my comments to Mr. B.

"If you would let Darrell make some decisions of his own—"

Darrell, perceiving me as an ally now, suddenly was able to communicate his feelings with no difficulty. He accused his parents of having an "advertising mentality."

"We don't talk," he said, "because the minute I disagree with you, the talk ends. I get a lecture. So what's the point?"

It was obvious to both parents that Darrell was telling them something about themselves that they ought to listen to. Because they really were enlightened and had his best interests at heart, they listened as he told them he didn't want to go to summer tennis camp, he didn't want to be on the tennis team, he didn't want to be a school jock and top scholar. He just wanted to "be a normal person."

That wasn't such a bad ambition, I ventured to say. And not surprisingly, Mr. and Mrs. B. said they agreed.

In the coming months, Mr. B. made a valiant and largely successful effort to get off his son's "case." When summertime arrived, Darrell got a job at a local gas station, and brought home a weekly paycheck, part of which he paid to his mother in rent. He managed to save a certain proportion, and by the end of the summer he had bought an expensive electric guitar and was practicing on it regularly several hours a day.

Darrell did not go out for the tennis team in the fall. Nobody asked him why, and he didn't volunteer to give any reasons. I think it was accepted that whatever his reasons were, they were his own, and he didn't have to explain to anyone. He did get together with a couple of other kids who had guitars, and they managed to play some pretty decent (if loud) rock music together.

What became very noticeable was that Darrell began to "open up" with the family, discussing some of his ambitions which, at least for the moment, were very much involved with playing music. There was a noticeable increased willingness on his part to take on job responsibilities around the house, and his manner generally was more cooperative and friendly. When therapy was discontinued after the first few weeks of school that following fall, members of the family were much more at ease with one another, and Darrell gave every indication of being ready for a successful year.

Practical Steps

The case of Darrell B. is instructive because it touches upon the majority, if not all, of the factors we have discussed pertaining to non-communication. Both parents desired to be helpful and supportive to their son. Yet, Darrell's father, by trying to manage every aspect of his son's life, was interfering and not allowing him to become his own person. Darrell's mother, with the best of intentions, was attempting to probe into areas of her son's inner-most feelings before he had sorted his feelings out sufficiently to share them with an adult. Not being able to verbalize his need for privacy, Darrell tended to react angrily to his parents, thus causing them to feel resentful and angry, too. Both sides had arrived at an impasse in communicating.

I. Be a listener

I cannot emphasize too much how important it is to really *listen* to your teen-ager. Listening implies more than hearing spoken words. Darrell's father heard, but he didn't listen. You may think you have all the answers, and indeed, it may actually be true, you *really do know* what is best and right for your child. But if your child is not ready to accept what is best and right at any particular time, then your gratuitous advice can be misunderstood, resented, and result in a closing off of communication.

Aside from control or disciplinary situations, *unsolicited advice* is better kept to yourself.

—"What do you want to hang out with that kid for, when so-and-so down the street is much nicer?"

—"If you wear your hair a certain way it makes you look a lot prettier."

—"Talk nice to adults, and they'll do more for you."

Forget that kind of advice. Your kid probably knows you are right, but doesn't want to hear it from you.

Your teen-ager has reached a point in life when he wants to solve things for himself. It is right for you to *listen*; your kid may be trying to tell you something; and from listening you will learn a lot about your kid. But *don't volunteer a lot of advice unless asked.* And don't, for heaven's sake, presume to ask personal questions of your kid. Darrell felt that his mother was trying to *pry*.

Maybe, eventually, teen-agers will tell you what's on their mind. And if they don't? Their right to inner privacy should not be violated.

II. Give your kid some control

Your teen-ager is at a period of his life when almost anything he does is a new experience. Sex, driving a car, getting a first summer job. There are a lot of choices involved in all of these areas, each one of which thrills and challenges your teen-ager as much as it terrifies you. If you always can be counted on to refuse your kid permission to do those things that are suddenly presented to him, sooner or later your kid will stop asking you for your permission or opinion.

Saying "yes" to a teen-ager can be the hardest thing a parent has to do. Yet, whenever possible, I urge parents to allow their kids to decide for themselves. Obviously, there are instances when parents must step in and exercise some control. In those instances, parents should be *as tactful as possible.* If your kid seems open to discussing his or her participation in what you consider to be a taboo activity, try to get your child to consider the pros and cons. By allowing him to weigh the matter for himself, you may be able to avoid the necessity of an outright rejection, while giving your teen-ager an opportunity to sort out his own opinion on the matter. If, as a last resort, you have to step in with your veto power, at least your kid will know what the various arguments are. And maybe—just maybe—

after all the facts are laid out on the table, you may even come to change your *own* mind; you may conclude that your kid's proposal isn't all that terrible, after all.

III. Keep an open mind

This matter of coming around to seeing a problem or making a decision from the same point of view as your children is not something to dismiss lightly. There is no better way for you to convince your kid that you are on his side than by coming around to his point of view. *I do not mean that you should give in when you think that something is wrong.* But oftentimes something that at first you tend to think is wrong, on reflection, may turn out not to be. If your kid really believes that you are open to reason, he will be more likely to listen to your point of view when you disagree with him. An inflexible domineering, controlling, standoffish, or critical stance toward your kid is a sure way to keep him at bay.

IV. Let them know that you're human, too

Your children have thought of you for the first 13 years of their lives as the all powerful (hopefully) benevolent dictator. Now they are beginning to re-examine some long-held attitudes. More than likely they will tend to see you still as a dictator, but not necessarily as benevolent. Children don't think of their parents as having experienced the same kinds of problems and choices that they are facing. A father lecturing his son about, "When I was your age," etc., is not the same as a father levelling and confessing to his kids that the time he stood up to the plate with the bases loaded, he hit into a double play, and the whole school treated him like a nerd for the next two weeks. Hearing this from your own lips may delight your child even more than you wanted it to, but it will have the virtue, at least, of letting him know that "old hard pants" once had a moment of being human, too.

V. Relax

As difficult as it may be for you to be confronted suddenly by a taciturn teen-ager, just remember that your kid is probably having a harder time of it than you are. For the various reasons we have seen, it is quite common for teen-agers to go through a period of limited communication, especially with their parents. You may wonder whatever happened to that charming little kid who used to run to you with every little scratched elbow, and come to you for advice on what to do about Johnny or Sarah next door who weren't "playing fair." For certain, those days are over. Your kid is trying to solve his own problems—*as he should*—and as unattractive as your kid may appear to be during this period, it is a passage that must be gone through. The best you can do to help him get through it is to relax and try to understand it. It may take awhile, but remember, your kid, too, is as anxious as you are to cross over from childhood to adulthood. The wait during the time that it is happening will be worth it when one day, almost magically, your teen-ager, perhaps upon returning home after being away for a term at college, or from a brief vacation trip, or from a summer job out-of-town, will look you in the eye and suddenly flash you that same wonderful smile you remember he used to give you when he was just a little fellow, as he says: "Hi, Mom. Hi, Dad. It's nice to be home again."

Problem #7

ⵯⵯⵯⵯⵯⵯⵯⵯⵯⵯⵯⵯⵯⵯⵯⵯⵯⵯⵯⵯⵯⵯⵯⵯⵯⵯⵯⵯⵯⵯ

"My Kid Doesn't Have Any Friends"

All parents want their kids to be popular. Popular kids seem to be a vindication of all the early years of support that parents have given and the effort they have made in raising their kids. One of the most successful TV situation comedies of a few years back was about teen-agers and was called "Happy Days." The kids in this sitcom were a happy bunch who were always *together*, and they did all the wonderful sappy, lovable and happy things that we like to think teen-agers should be doing. Sure, they had their little disagreements and disappointments, but everything always worked out fine in the end. That's the way we would like it to be for all of our kids.

Popularity is as American as apple pie and ice

cream. As the character Willy Loman stressed to his son Biff in Arthur Miller's classic American play, *Death of a Salesman*, it is important "to be well-liked." Being well-liked is a prescription for *success*. When in Willy's case the prescription didn't work, his life ended in tragedy. Audiences empathized with Willy's failed dreams, and openly wept at the tragic events on stage.

Prior to the teen-age years, it is oftentimes difficult to detect whether a child is popular with other children. Unless the pre-adolescent is openly hostile and is abusive or aggressive to other members of the peer group, small children tend to accept more or less unquestioningly the companionship of those around them. True, they have their squabbles, and they form cliques, but the alignments keep changing, and usually there is no clear pattern of either social acceptance or isolation. During these early years *parents* are the popular leaders with pre-teens, the role of the parent being to bring small children together, arrange birthday parties, chauffeur kids around to other kids' houses, and conduct excursion trips over week-ends.

During the teen-age years, however, when kids are developing individual identities and move into a phase of making plans for themselves, they tend to look upon their peers much more critically and selectively. And because they know that they themselves are being looked at, they make efforts to accommodate to what their peers expect of them.

How well this process of accommodation and selection proceeds is the determining factor in the popularity of teen-age children. It does not take long for parents to observe how their kids are doing in the accommodation and selection process.

What Parents Observe

As your child approaches the teen-age years, you notice many changes that are taking place, and you are curious to see how well your child measures up to his or her peers. Likely as not, you cherish some preconceived notions having to do with groups of noisy but likable kids congregating in the kitchen of your house for raids on the refrigerator before withdrawal to the family room, or to your child's room, for relaxation and conversation around the stereo.

When the kids don't show up at your house, but instead tend to congregate in the house of the kid living next door (that rather "ordinary" kid who for years has been your kid's best friend), and, in fact, your youngster all of a sudden is not even invited to join them now, you experience your first twinge of concern.

Perhaps you are able to put your concern behind you, with the idea that the kid next door "never was very much anyway." There are plenty of other kids for your kid to link up with.

But, then, at the fall semester conference with your child's teachers you are told that your child seems to "hang back," that your child is not participating in any school activities. You learn that in the opinion of your teachers your child is shy, or perhaps even a "loner" who doesn't seem to make friends easily.

Well, you tell yourself, your kid is self-reliant, and doesn't need to have a lot of friends. And you may be right. But, as very often happens with kids who are not making friends easily during the teen-age years, your child may begin to lean more on *you* to supply interest in his young life. Suddenly you find that your teen-ager, instead of going through a period of independence from you, is actually looking to you for support more than ever before. You become aware that the demands of your kid on your time are becoming somewhat cloying.

"Aren't you lucky!" says the parent of that popular kid next door. His kid is so popular that he seems to have no time at all for his parents.

Chances are you don't know whether you are lucky or not. You wish your kid was going off with the gang, and not hanging around so much with Mommy in the kitchen, or with Daddy in the garage. You like taking your boy or girl out to a restaurant with you once in awhile, but not every time you go out.

"Your child is so adult," say your admiring friends when they see how well-behaved he is at adult social functions. And you are pleased—kind of. But deep down you cannot help but wonder if your "adult" child, as a result of his hanging around with adults so much, is not simply putting off his own adult development by avoiding the necessary adult process of accommodation and natural selection with his peers.

Perhaps even more disturbing to parents is the teen-ager who because he has no friends will tend to withdraw from social activity altogether. Teenagers who feel keenly the pain of rejection oftentimes suffer a concomitant loss in self-esteem. The child feels like a failure, a social misfit. Their feelings of worthlessness oftentimes carry over into their schoolwork, and they begin to bring home poor grades. Kids with low self esteem tend to gravitate to other kids with low self esteem, and together there is a danger that they will turn to drugs and other socially undesirable habits.

Some lonely kids turn to eating too much, and become overweight, thus making themselves more unattractive, and at the same time furnishing themselves with an excuse as to why they are unpopular.

"I have this weight problem, see, and the kids don't like me, because I can't move as fast as they can."

There are always exceptions, of course. Sometimes the shy or socially uncomfortable child will turn his or her energies to constructive efforts, seeking approval by becoming a "brain," an artist, a brilliant comic, a scientist, a philosopher. Despite their difficulties in fitting in socially, such children have strong egos that prevent them from losing their basic high self esteem. They have an underlying faith in their own worth, despite seeming evidence to the contrary. Oftentimes when they reach adulthood they accomplish extraordinary achievements in life.

But whatever the form the child's unpopularity takes, the parent of the teen-age child who is not making friends cannot help but be concerned. And in their concern, parents will oftentimes try to act as "social directors" over their children's lives. They try to set up situations where their kids can meet and mingle with other teen-age kids. They push their kids forward, trying to get them to make new friends. When these efforts fail, as they usually do, the disappointment that they feel is considerable.

"What is wrong with my kid?" is the question

most often posed to me by parents whose children do not have any friends.

Parents whose sons and daughters shy away from members of the opposite sex will sometimes wonder if their children have homosexual inclinations. It is very common for children who are not relating easily to the peer group as a whole to lavish attention exclusively on just one other person of the same sex. Such attachments can cause parents real concern.

Parents whose teen-age children do not fit in easily with other teen-agers sometimes lose patience with their children. The disappointment that the parents feel (often having to do with unfulfilled vicarious ambitions of their own) can be very apparent to the troubled teen-ager, with the result that the feelings of inadequacy that the child already feels are exacerbated, and an unhappy situation is made even worse.

Why Some Kids Have No Friends

The teen-age years are a time of change. Children who only a year or two before were content to play bicycle tag or make dresses for their dolls now look on these activities as "childish" or beneath them. As their interests change, they change the selection of their friends. A girl who suddenly develops into a popular sexy campus queen may no longer have much in common with the girl who is not very attractive, but a whiz in science. The boy who is a talented guitarist may have very little in common with his former buddy, now the baseball star. All of these teen-agers, with their rapidly developing individual interests, will be gravitating toward new friends who seem to share some part of their own changed, new vision of life.

For the teen-ager the process of finding out where he or she fits in is not always an easy one. Let's look for a moment at kids who don't appear to have this problem at all, the kids who are the sports stars and the beauty queens. It often seems that our society values glamor more than anything else. The lives and lifestyles of the rich and famous interest us. Magazines such as PEOPLE feature the "private" lives of movie stars and the so-called "beautiful people." Teen-age children who are handsome or particularly talented in some area that captures the current popular fancy of the teen-age culture have no trouble attracting other teen-agers to themselves.

Popularity arising from one's good looks or campus achievements is not necessarily, however, an indication of how many *real friends* a teen-ager has. Like adults, the "popular" figure oftentimes finds himself surrounded by sycophants, people who hope that some of the reflected glamor of the popularity figure may rub off onto themselves.

There is a reverse side of this equation, too. People who are popular oftentimes *bask in the glory* of their popularity, collecting "friends" and showing them off like a collection of trinkets. Friends who are collected like objects of material value to be discarded when their usefulness or novelty wears off are not true friends. Teen-agers, or anyone else, for that matter, who use others to enhance their own image are following a pattern described by psychologists as *narcissism*. There are varying degrees of narcissism, of course, but the classic narcissistic personality is one that indicates a basic inner emptiness, reflecting an underdevelopment of genuine feelings of self worth. In order to compensate and to ward off depressive feelings, such kids are often driven to collect people to buttress their sagging self esteem. These kids usually manifest a false heartiness, or a compulsive flirtatiousness. Having lots of boys chasing after you, all of whom hope to "score," is not popularity; it is desperation.

Real friends are an important part of the development of an adolescent. When teen-agers find their own particular circle of friends they are on the way toward defining to themselves (and to the world) who they are. "Birds of a feather flock together" is the common saying, and it is true for teen-agers especially. Teen-agers tend to gravitate toward others who share their interests.

But this process of teen-age "peer bonding" is not an instant or necessarily easy process. Which is why I caution parents not to expect their kids to be too popular too soon. If your kid does not fit easily into the popular "in" group, or "clique," there can be a number of reasons for it.

Your kid *may not be ready yet* to take his place among his peers. Either he doesn't know yet just where his real interests lie, or he may think that he knows but is still too shy to test himself. Not all kids develop physiologically at the same rate as they do chronologically. A boy whose voice has changed and has sprouted pubic hair may be ready to test himself with girls, whereas a boy of the same age who has not yet reached puberty may be terrified to *even talk* to girls.

The matter of finding the *right* group is key, of course, for every kid. And this takes time. The kid who cannot find friends whom he likes or who like him may be trying to fit in with a group that he really has no natural affinity for. Oftentimes these are kids who *think they ought* to be associated with a particular group that they have nothing in common with. I once worked with a boy who weighed 140 pounds, was skinny as a rail, and was clumsy, who desperately wanted to be accepted by the jocks on the football team. He couldn't play football himself, and he wasn't particularly the mascot or comic type. In fact, he had nothing in common at all with the guys on the football team. What he most liked to do was to write poems! Somewhere along the line, possibly as the result of having watched too many beer commercials on television, he thought he couldn't be happy if he wasn't "in" with the guys on the football team.

Not every kid is going to make as many friends as every other kid. Some kids will find only one or two others with whom they share a common attitude toward life. Particularly in the age range of from 13 to 15, sometimes a kid for a time will form an intense friendship with just one other kid of the same sex. Almost as if common blood flows between them, they seem inseparable. To the adult onlooker they appear to be both secretive and childish; just about anything that one says to the other turns out to be a complete riot. They are always disappearing to a secluded part of the house or off somewhere where you can't see them in the backyard. Very often they will try to look alike, buying identical clothes. Whether they look alike or not, they certainly make every effort to *act* alike.

Is this form of social relating abnormal, many parents ask me? On the contrary, holding onto an exclusive friendship can be a healthy way of a kid's protecting himself from the often awesome and terrifying normative expectations of teen-age life. For the slightly immature teen, an exclusive friend allows some breathing space from the demands of going to basketball games, or hanging out with a group of kids whom he is not ready to join yet, or who don't interest him. Having an exclusive friend can preserve for a time an important illusion of sameness and certainty at a time in the teen-ager's life when everything from the past seems to be slipping away. What a relief it is for the teen-ager to be able to spend every bit of spare time with someone who behaves like himself, values what he values, and gives him a feeling of total acceptance and safety *all the time*. A close friend validates the teenager's own view of life while preparing him for the next step in life, which is to develop additional friends, or different intensities of friendships with a variety of people, ranging from the casual to deeply loyal.

Some teen-age kids go through a period of not even having one friend. These are the veritable loners, among whom we find the deep thinkers, the philosophers, as it were. They spend long hours contemplating their place in the world, or wondering even if they have a place. This is the kind of kid who keeps parents awake all night with worry.

The teen-ager who is a loner oftentimes is going through a very important step in his particular growing up process, a process that involves his trying to find out which group, if any, he belongs in. It's possible that for the time being he may conclude that he doesn't really fit in with any particular group.

In time, many loners change, becoming less

threatened by relationships, more trusting of others, and perhaps even finding it within themselves to lower unreasonably high standards so as to find a group of friends, or at least one or two close friends.

On the other hand, if your son or daughter is extremely sensitive and prone to deep thought, he or she may maintain a distance from peers for a longer period of time, possibly even a lifetime. It is important to realize that *this is not necessarily a bad thing*. The important thing is that your teen-ager is happy or contented with the particular relationship to life that he or she has formed. It is a mistake to try to push a loner teen-ager into relationships that he or she is not ready for, or does not want or need. If our own view of happiness is associated in our minds with group popularity, that is well and good, as long as we do not try to foist this view of life onto our children who may not share the same view. The main task of adolescence—and maybe of the whole of life itself—is to find out who we are, and to follow the beat of our own drum. If there is something positive about us that is unique, separate from the group, we should nurture it, and let it grow and flourish within. Unless a person can divest himself of the desire to be what he isn't, unless he can let go of some of the externally imposed standards which bear little resemblance to his inner core, he will remain unhappy and quite possibly alienated from himself and others throughout his entire life.

Every so often I run across a youngster who might be described as a "friendless individual," a kid who is something of the class reject, the outcast, the belittled person, the "nerd." Think back to your own playground days, and you will probably recall that there was always one kid who was the butt of the others, the kid who was teased either because he walked funny, looked funny, talked funny, or simply projected an aura of being a "weirdo." There seemed to be no hope for this child. He rarely found any defenders among the hecklers, and even among the more sensitive non-hecklers, no one was ever willing to intervene on his behalf.

To be on the receiving end of cruel jibes can be one of the most humiliating and frustrating experiences of adolescence. There is no winning in these circumstances; attempts to retaliate by the beleaguered kid are ineffective against the overwhelming force of the tormenting crowd; and to ignore the tormenters is only to invite intensified and escalated assaults.

What brings about the phenomenon of the group attack on one individual? It seems to me that human beings in this situation are compelled to follow the same dictates of nature that other species of the animal kingdom follow. The weak animal in the pack is oftentimes attacked by the others. This anthropomorphic comparison of human with animal behavior is valid, I think, and probably is deeply rooted in the compelling need for animal creatures to weed out the weaker specimens to ensure survival of the species. Unlike animals, we humans are able to make a choice ultimately between civilized behavior and primal behavior, but particularly on the teen-age level (and sometimes on the adult level, too) the civilized sense is not always as developed as it might be.

In my experience, the outcast kid carries along with him an aura of weakness, or more precisely, defenselessness. This is borne out, I think, in our literature which is rife with stories about the tormented outsider who secretly takes boxing or judo lessons and one day turns on the leading bully of the pack, and knocks him to the ground. Having thus asserted his own value and strength, the former "weirdo" is then accepted into the inner circle.

There used to be ads for Charles Atlas body building equipment in which the skinny "99-pound weakling" had sand kicked in his face by a handsome muscular brute who walked away with the weakling's girlfriend. (I used to hate the girlfriend for being so disloyal.) After several months of using Charles Atlas's dynamic tension spring devices, the former weakling went back to the beach, beat up the bully, and reclaimed his girl.

Unfortunately, the outcast kids I have seen usually have not taken the steps necessary to extricate themselves from the loser role they have been cast in. I am not suggesting that they should take body building so they can beat up the bullies (though body building might very well be a sign of strength that the bullies ultimately would respect). I am suggesting that the picked-on kid needs to do something to make himself less defenseless.

The reason this particular kind of kid is helpless, I believe, is because the kid has no inner resource of self respect. The youngster feels like a loser to begin with, and brings this with him into the arena of teen-age jockeying for position and self definition. Where does this low self esteem originate?

Very often I find that the outcast kid has a feeling that *his own parents do not really fully approve of him.* In some families, where there are two children, one may be favored at the other's expense because the first child is charming, charismatic, independent, athletic, highly intelligent, or even of a different sex; the outcast child may exhibit traits that the family does not highly prize such as timidity, demandingness, awkwardness, physical unattractiveness, or clumsiness. Sometimes very subtly (and sometimes quite blatantly), parents will show their disapproval of or disappointment with the latter youngster, thereby setting off feelings in the child of unworthiness.

Youngsters who enter the teen-age years feeling uncomfortable about themselves are prime targets for other stronger teen-agers, all of whom are struggling to find their positions in the world. Parents who no doubt unwittingly have helped create this situation have a heavy burden of responsibility in helping the teen-ager to restore his or her sense of self worth.

Helping the Teen-ager Without Friends

You can tell a kid to stop smoking pot, or to stop lying, or to start becoming responsible, or to work harder in school, and it may or may not work. But one thing is sure, you can't tell a kid to "be popular" and expect it to be at all helpful. Kids have to *learn* how to cope with the world by living with other kids and through the process of accommodation and selection define for themselves where their particular social niche is and where they fit in. Sometimes a bit of *guidance* can be helpful, as for example by directing a child into certain areas where it appears his or her strengths lie. But most of all, you can be helpful by offering an understanding ear and by being supportive of your child as he or she goes through the painful times of rejection and the joyful times of acceptance.

Before we look at some practical steps that parents can take to help their teen-ager we will look at the case history of one particularly unhappy child who could not make friends.

CASE STUDY—TIMMY F.

The Complaint

"He's a wonderful boy," Mrs. F. told me almost immediately after she and her husband and Timmy had sat down in my office the first time.

"Oh, yes," Mr. F. agreed.

And then both parents proceeded to describe their son further as "lacking in self-confidence, possessing a poor self-image, having no friends, and being too dependent on his parents."

Timmy was an extremely handsome, sandy-haired youngster of 14 years, with a somewhat serious expression, but with a mischievous gleam in his eye, too. It was hard to believe that this was a young man who was having trouble making friends. Yet, when it was his turn to speak, he mostly confirmed the opinion of his parents.

"I'm boring," he volunteered. "Nobody likes me, because I'm an introvert, and don't fit in." Seeing that he had found a sympathetic ear, he went on to say that the other kids picked on him, even though he never did anything to provoke them. It was a shock to hear this good-looking, well-built boy talking about being picked on and harassed, and passing himself off as a hopeless "loser." He wasn't kidding, either. It was obvious that he felt badly about himself and about his relationships with the kids at school.

As Timmy talked, I couldn't help notice that Mr. F.'s forehead was furrowing into a frown.

"Does it disturb you to hear your son describe himself in these terms?" I asked him.

"Yes it does, frankly," he replied. "He goes around as though he were looking for ways to set himself to be knocked down. I don't know why he does that."

To which Timmy replied, "They're all jerks, anyway. I don't like being around them. They're all hypocrites, one minute being okay, and the next minute showing their true colors."

Whether he really *did not like* being around his peers, or whether he was *afraid* to be around his peers I couldn't tell at first. What I did learn soon, however, was that Timmy relied very heavily on his parents for social intercourse. After school, instead of going to a friend's house, Timmy would hang around his mother. Mostly he would ask her for advice about how to handle one or more of the knotty interpersonal problems he had had with the kids at school that day. One of the activities that he looked forward to every day was helping his mother in the kitchen.

It did not take long for Mrs. F. to blurt out in one of our sessions that she really didn't like Timmy helping her in the kitchen, and she really didn't like having him put the burden of solving his peer problems at school on her. She confessed that sometimes when she would make suggestions to help Timmy he would strongly disagree with her. This would tend to annoy both of them, leading to some fairly bitter arguments.

A similar scenario would be enacted almost daily between Timmy and Mr. F. Timmy would request help after dinner with his homework. However, when Mr. F. would make the effort to help him, Timmy would only pay half-hearted attention, keeping one ear cocked at the stereo while his father did the lion's share of the actual work. Once more an argument would break out. Mr. and Mrs. F. said that because they were as concerned as they were about Timmy they hesitated to leave him alone when they went out. Like a piece of luggage, they dragged him around with them wherever they went—to the ice cream parlor, out to dinner, to sporting events.

What it seemed to me that we were observing here was a catch-22 situation. On the one hand, Timmy was troubled by his apparent inability to make friends at school. On the other hand, he was relying more and more on his parents for a social outlet, the result being that some irritation was growing between the parents and their son at home, as well. In other words, Timmy seemed to be alienating people in all areas of his life.

Background

AT 14, Timmy was the "baby" in a family of three children, the other two being older sisters, both of whom were now in college. Timmy's relationship with his sisters had always been somewhat strained. His oldest sister, Leslie, was a fierce competitor and high achiever in school. His other sister, Janet, was not as ambitious as Leslie, but was the family pride and joy, and popular favorite with both her peers and teachers.

Both Mr. and Mrs. F. were intelligent and career-minded parents. Mr. F. was a marketing vice president in a computer manufacturing company, and Mrs. F. held a position of importance in an advertising agency. Both of them expected a great deal from their children, although in the children's earlier years, the parents were not always available to give them a great deal of support. Both daughters managed to live up to the expectations of Mr. and Mrs. F. But Timmy, the son they both wanted to be the next generation standard bearer of the family, seemed somehow to be lacking in drive.

"I *can't stand* a kid that won't try!" Mr. F. exploded at one of our early sessions.

Mrs. F. held a somewhat similar attitude. "My greatest fear," she said one day, "is that he'll be helplessly dependent all his life."

Reaching Understanding

What I was hearing in the exchanges between parents and son in this particular family was that the parents were very disappointed in their son. The impression I got was that the disappointment was not only over the fact that Timmy could not make friends or that he demanded too much of their time to compensate for his lonely state, but that they simply did not feel he was going to measure up to their expectations—*and they had felt this way for a long time.* He was not even measuring up to the performance of his sisters.

While making many attempts to help Timmy, Mr. and Mrs. F. failed to recognize their own disappointment in him. Timmy simply was not the same as his sisters, and was not proceeding along toward adulthood as smoothly as the other children. This "lack" in their son inwardly annoyed them. What they did not see was that Timmy keenly sensed their disappointment, and in fact, *expected them to display their annoyance toward him.* He would hang around his mother in the kitchen and "help" her, just waiting for her to become annoyed with him. He would ask his father for help with his homework, but pay minimal attention, just waiting for his father to become annoyed with him. The result was that when both parents revealed their feelings, it seemed to confirm to Timmy that he was an unworthy person.

It was the burden of this low estimation of himself that Timmy carried with him everywhere he went, including in his daily appearances at school. Because he basically did not believe that he was a "likable" person he unconsciously would find ways to expose the "hypocrisy" of *everybody* with whom he came in contact.

For example, Timmy would go out of his way to make friends with the "jocks" at school by taking part in intramural touch football games. When he fumbled the ball repeatedly, the other kids criticized him, at which point he took the criticism very personally, had his expectations confirmed, and stalked off the field in a huff. It was no wonder that the other kids began to treat him as something of a "nerd."

Creative Synthesis

To help Timmy make new friends and to enable him to lessen his reliance on Mr. and Mrs. F., it was necessary to take a two-pronged approach.

First, with regard to Timmy and his parents, I pointed out to Mr. and Mrs. F. that the real reason why they were spending so much time and effort working at being his "social planner" was that they really had very little faith in their son. They were worrying about his ability to function socially, primarily because they didn't really have a very high regard for his particular personality, which was so different from his sisters'. The result was that they were helping to undermine his confidence at the same time as they were resenting the time they were spending with him. They would be doing Timmy a favor, as well as themselves, I said, if they would *stop worrying* about him. They weren't helping Timmy by trying to fill in his social life through their own efforts.

To Mrs. F., I said, "You are afraid that Timmy will be dependent on you all his life, and everything you do contributes to making him more dependent. It's really a kind of contempt you have for him."

Mr. F. interjected and confessed that he had long wanted to get out of the "social planning business," but had deferred to his wife who was the "worrier" in the family.

"Stop *worrying* about me!" Timmy shot back. "You think I'm helpless because I'm not like Leslie!"

"You don't have to be like Leslie," Mr. F. replied somewhat sheepishly.

"Do you really mean that?" I put in.

"All I want is for him to be happy," Mr. F. answered.

"Then, let's give him a chance to be himself," I said.

"From now on I'm going to go about my business, and he can do the same," Mr. F. said.

"Well, let's try it that way," I said. "I think everyone might feel better."

Next, with his parents absent, Timmy and I set out to organize a program for him to make new friends. It was difficult convincing Timmy that he was a "likable" person, but I pointed out to him that, for example, I myself liked him very much. He was the kind of person, I said, that most people would be happy to have for a friend. He was intelligent, good-looking, had a good sense of humor, enjoyed outdoor sports—who wouldn't like a boy like that.

When he continued to express some doubts, I suggested that rather than set out to "make a friend" (somebody who might turn out to be a "hypocrite"), he ought simply to look around to see if there wasn't somebody who, on a limited basis, he might like to do something with that they both could enjoy. He agreed this wasn't a bad idea, and after two weeks of "window shopping," he got up his nerve to ask another boy to go skiing with him.

The skiing trip went well, and the following week the boy reciprocated, and invited Timmy to go skiing.

Meanwhile, Timmy decided to "put a little distance" between himself and the "jocks" who had been tormenting him, and who, he admitted, didn't have much in common with him, anyway. He took up a new extra-curricular activity—break dancing—

which he enjoyed, and apparently was quite good at. Within three weeks, one of the girls in the break dance group invited *him* to go on a ski week-end, with her parents along in charge and as chaperones.

After that week-end, Timmy boasted to me that he had a "girl friend." Although he was afraid that other people, including his parents, might not approve because she wasn't "good-looking," he said he liked her anyway, and he was making plans to go skiing with her again.

"What other people think isn't important," I told Timmy. "If this is a nice girl, and you like her, that's the only thing that's important. You are doing what *you* want to do, not what you think somebody else expects of you."

Timmy liked hearing this. It made him feel that his own judgment was worthwhile. He asked the girl to go skiing with him, and asked his own parents to take them.

Was this asking his parents to be social directors of his life, he wanted to know?

Absolutely not, I told him. Approaching his parents for a favor so that he could conduct his social life was quite a different thing from asking them to *fulfill* his social life by entertaining him.

Whatever Timmy's parents may have thought about his new girl friend, they were sensitive enough not to reveal by word or gesture anything of a disappointment. In fact, they seemed genuinely delighted to find out that their son actually liked a girl who liked him in return. This was precisely the attitude they needed to have if Timmy was to feel good about himself.

And Timmy *was* beginning to feel better about himself, and to realize that he could make friends, just like everyone else. Once this attitude became a fixed part of him, he almost forgot about how he had been picked on before. Six months later, when therapy was discontinued, Timmy had several friends whom he felt good about, and who felt good about him.

Practical Steps

Nobody can make friends for another person. What parents *can* do to help a teen-ager who is having difficulty in making friends is to try to determine the underlying problems that are getting in the youngster's way.

I. Let your kid know you like him

Teen-agers are not always lovable. They can be moody, disrespectful, sloppy, irresponsible, and a hundred other things that make them not pleasant to be around. But you know all this already. If you truly are disappointed in your teen-ager, if in fact, you really *don't like* the direction your teen-ager kid is moving in, you may be conveying signals of the kind that say, "You are an unlikable person." This was precisely what was happening in the case of Timmy F., and why Timmy felt he couldn't make friends.

You don't have to approve or even like all of the behavior patterns of your teen-ager. But if you find yourself at a point where in all honesty you have to admit that you don't like very much the kind of kid your teen-ager is turning into, then you should face up to this squarely. Decide what it is about your kid that you don't like. If you can come up with some honest answers, you should then take the next step and determine if your expectations are unrealistic.

Is it because your daughter isn't a boy and can't play football that you suddenly realize you are disappointed in her?

Is your son a mathematical whiz who loves to create programs on his personal computer when what you really want is for him to *hate* math, as you did, and become a poet (which you didn't).

Do you have one child who is the apple of your eye whom you favor over another?

If the answer to any of the above—or to any questions that are *similar* to the above—is "yes," you may be making it difficult for your child to make friends. My advice in such a case is to *get rid* of your own cherished pre-conceived notions of what you would like your child to be. Then look at and respect those qualities in your child that are truly his or her own. This is the way to give your children the confidence they need to go into the world of their peers and make friends that they can hold.

If you have more than one child, each may be very different. But they all have their own special qualities. At various times one or another of the children may need more help or guidance or understanding—even more time and attention—than another, but at no time and under no circumstances should you *favor* one child over another. The children should all understand that you are even-handed to the best of your ability. As long as they know that deep-down you love them equally for their own inner qualities, they will be confident in the world of their peers, and succeed in making and holding friends.

II. Avoid being critical

The last thing that a teen-ager who doesn't have any friends needs is *criticism* about it from his parents. Obviously, the child is feeling low already. Everybody wants and needs some kind of friendship. Pushing a child to be more "outgoing," or ridiculing a child for not making more effort, will oftentimes cause a child to withdraw even further from the social arena.

Just because a child seems to have no friends, it does not mean that the child will never have any friends. Teen-agers go through periods of introspection and self-doubt as they jockey for position in the social world. If your child seems to be something of a loner, don't criticize his behavior. Try to find out what your child's particular interests are, and encourage him or her to pursue those interests. Chances are in the course of doing those things that are most meaningful to them, they will automatically become friends with kids who have similar interests. Timmy F. found his closest friends through his interests in skiing and break dancing.

III. Don't criticize the few friends that your child has

The loner kid oftentimes will break out of his lonely period by bringing home one day a new friend who may at first appear to be as lonely and as sad as your own kid. Although you may not be overly impressed with this new friend, you should make every effort to encourage the friendship.*

If your kid sees something valuable in another

---

*Obviously, if the new friend has bad habits, such as being into drugs, etc., you have to have a serious discussion with your child. See Problem #8, "My Kid Is Hanging Out With a Bad Crowd."

kid who may not look like your own idea of a "proper" friend, your child may be seeing things that you are missing in life. What is it in the new youngster—whether of the same sex or opposite sex—that appeals to your teen-ager? What have you missed seeing in your own child that makes him or her gravitate to this new friend?

Remember, a criticism of your child's friend is, in a sense, a criticism of your child, too. As hard as it may be for you to accept, your child may be getting more understanding from his new friend whom you disapprove of than he is getting from you. You may still be seeing your child as you would like him to be, rather than as he is developing. In such cases, your child will tend to trust his friend more than he trusts you. By opposing the friendship, you are driving a wedge between yourself and your child.

IV. Avoid being a social planner

If your teen-age child is unable to enter successfully into the social arena, it doesn't help for you to try to push him in. It is understandable that you should feel anxious when a child fails to negotiate a developmental hurdle. But if you force your child into a social situation because of your own anxiety, and the child fails, the consequences can be devastating in terms of the humiliation experienced. When your child is ready to make a friend, he will. Your interfering is only a signal that you have no faith or trust in your child, and makes him all the more uncertain.

If your child is having trouble making friends, it is just possible that he or she is looking for friends in the wrong places. Timmy F., for example, was much happier with his break dance friends than he was with the football "jocks." These are matters for your teen-ager to decide for himself.

You should be on guard against unconscious subtle ways of pushing your child into areas where he does not feel most comfortable. Take the case, for example, of the family that takes out a membership for their child in the local country club. The child may feel obliged to go and spend time by the pool or on the golf links when, in fact, what he most wants to do is to play his drums to the accompaniment of some new hard rock records that he has bought. At the club, the child may not be able to make friends with the kids simply because they are the kinds of kids who enjoy being there. Wise, indeed, are the parents who recognize at an early point that even with the best of intentions they have been steering their child into unfriendly waters.

Problem #8

~~~~~~

"My Kid Is Hanging Out with a Bad Crowd"

Parents are perhaps more worried today about the direction their kids are taking and the kinds of other kids they are "hanging out" with than ever before. And there is good reason for this. In today's world a bad crowd is associated in everybody's mind with one overriding concern: the nightmare of heavy drug use.

Drugs are everywhere. (An increase in the use of *alcohol* by teenagers has been noted by observers, too.) It is very likely today that if your kid is not a regular user of drugs, he or she has at least *tried* them, or at the *very least* been offered them by his or her peers.

The consequence of this "drug culture" that we live in is devastating to our teen-agers. Drugs (and alcohol) are directly associated daily with car fatalities, and an inexhaustible variety of anti-social behaviors, including larceny, drug-trafficking and homicides. Drugs and alcohol are directly or indirectly responsible for kids dropping out of school, for reduced job performance (and job related injuries) and jail. The fact is that drugs can erode the moral underpinnings and character of an entire society.*

According to David Toma, a rehabilitated drug and alcohol abuser, now a crusader for "Taking the High Out of High School,"* 25 teen-agers die each day (approximately 175 per week) in the United States as a result of drug or alcohol related accidents. Suicides, often associated with drug use, account for 100 deaths of teen-agers each week.

But parents don't need to be reminded of the statistics in order to have a healthy fearful respect for the drug dangers that face every teen-ager today. Daily we are made aware of celebrities and athletes who have been associated with drug use—most often these days with cocaine. Some have gone to jail; some have died from drug overdoses. At rock concerts and in municipal parks marijuana is now smoked in clear view of the police. The odor of marijuana smoke can be detected routinely in some movie theatres.

*Witness early 20th century China where the impoverished peasant class was hopelessly opium addicted, and more recently, in mid-Eastern nations where hashish is smoked quite openly in cafes. Interestingly, and perhaps something to be taken note of, the greatest social revolutionary upheavals of our time have taken place, or are in process of taking place, in these two widely separated geographical areas of the world.
*For information, write *The Changing Family*, WOR-TV, P.O. Box 9, Secaucus, N.J.

Moreover, drugs are no longer the exclusive domain of "hippies" or outsiders or underground radicals or rock musicians. All segments of teen-age society today are exposed to drugs. Drug use, one might say, is very democratic. It does not discriminate on the basis of race, religion, ethnic background, or even class. Thus, it is not easy for parents to determine quickly whether the gang their kid is hanging out with is "bad" or not. The clean-cut "jock" athlete may be as much, or more, of a heavy drug user than the scuffy kid in a jean jacket and long hair, a last remnant of the age of radical hippiedom.

Your First Suspicions

You can be reasonably sure that the first time your child experiments with drugs he or she is not going to come to you and ask your permission, or tell you all about it. Nevertheless, you probably will find out soon enough. One way or another.

Parents first detect signs of drug use on the part of their adolescents through a variety of ways. Very often they become suspicious as a result of a change in the teen-ager's habits—an actual personality change. The child may have difficulty getting up and going to school in the morning. Or perhaps the youngster appears at the dining room table one evening totally "bummed out." Or the child is suddenly hyper-active and over-communicative, in contrast to a normally quiet manner.

Most commonly, parents first become aware of adolescent drug use when they actually find paraphernalia or other evidence that their kids carelessly leave out in the open or in a purse or pocket of their clothes. It almost seems as though kids these days *want* their parents to know that they have reached the age when drugs are available to them. Thirty years ago every teen-age boy carried a rubber condom in his wallet until it deteriorated and fell apart from non-use. Today it is a hashish pipe or a quarter ounce of marijuana going stale in a plastic sandwich bag in an underwear drawer.

The kind of crowd a teen-ager hangs out with is a crucial factor in determining whether a child will become heavily involved with drugs. As noted already, superficial factors having to do with clothing "style," etc., are not necessarily the determining factors. Rather, if you learn that the crowd your child is hanging out with is getting into trouble locally, say as a result of stealing, or developing a bad reputation at school you may have reason to take close notice. Chances are that if your child is hanging out with a crowd known to be "bad apples" and drug users, sooner or later you will learn of your own child's drug use as a result of receiving a phone call from the school authorities or, worse, from the police.

The most common reaction of parents upon learning that their kid is involved in some way with drugs is to panic. The panic is then usually followed by a confrontation with the child in the presence of both parents. These confrontations are not always very successful. Invariably teen-agers will either deny using drugs or, if that doesn't work, they will try to play down the extent of their use of drugs. If pressed hard enough, teen-agers will often promise never to use drugs again. (Don't believe them.)

There then fellows typically a period when the parents go slightly "crazy." Very often one or both parents will feel that they "can't trust" their child anymore. As a result, they will resort to such ignominious behavior as secretly searching for evidence by opening their children's mail, rummaging through their soiled laundry, checking their bureau drawers, looking for dilation of the pupils in their eyes, etc., etc. It is not uncommon for panicky parents to threaten their children with jail or other institutionalization if they continue to be involved in any way with drugs.

Given the context of the culture that we live in and that I have touched on briefly, this panicky behavior on the part of the parents is certainly understandable, but it is mostly self-defeating, and rarely will have any positive effect on a child facing the choice of whether or not to become seriously involved with drug use.

The pertinent question for parents today is not so much, "Is my kid involved with drugs?" Rather, it is. "*To what extent* is my kid involved with drugs?"

Is our kid a *one-time* user?

Has your kid experimented as often as a *half-dozen times* with drugs?

Is your kid, though a non-user, keenly *aware* of drugs, and a friend of other kids who are users?

Is your kid a *heavy* user, either addicted already or on the road to addiction?

This section is designed to help guide those parents who are faced with either evidence or suspicion that their child is experimenting with drugs or is at a point in his or her life when the temptation to do so is very apparent. This section *does not address itself to the matter of treatment of drug* *addicted kids.* This section is designed to help parents deal with the difficult realization that their kids may be currently exposed to drug use, and to help them take steps that will work in time to *prevent* their kids from becoming addicted or heavy users of drugs.*

Why Kids Are Attracted to Drugs

Drugs and alcohol are everywhere today. In my experience, I can't think of a single kid that I know who has graduated from high school who hasn't at least experimented briefly with either beer, wine, hard liquor, or some form of controlled substance (marijuana still being the preferred choice today among the latter.)

Drugs today are a pervasive force in our culture. To expect kids not to be influenced by the culture of their time is as unrealistic as to believe in the tooth fairy. Our grandparents grew up in the prohibition era, and risked going blind drinking "bathtub gin." The fact that alcoholic beverages were illegal and that half the stuff that was served could poison them only served to make drinking more attractive. It was the "Flapper Age," and drinking was the "thing to do."

*Heavy drug use I define as habitual use to the extent that it interferes with one's normal functioning and well-being, and/or is a threat to the well-being of others. If your child is already into heavy drug use, my advice is to get professional help. There are a variety of approaches to solving heavy drug abuse problems. Family counseling, individual psychotherapy, drug rehabilitation clinics and community programs all can be helpful, depending on the individual situation and the individual relationship that parents have with their children. Specific therapeutic techniques and approaches to drug abuse have been developed, and there is good reason to be optimistic that in the right program your child can be rehabilitated.

During the years of World War II hundreds of thousands of teen-age GI's and home front defense workers became addicted to *cigarette smoking* largely as a result of advertising and free cartons of cigarettes sent to the war fronts by cigarette companies. There wasn't a War Bond billboard in those days that didn't feature a GI with a cigarette smoldering between his lips.

In the 1960's Civil Rights activists and anti-Vietnam war demonstrators burned their bras and their draft cards, and celebrated a new sexual freedom.

These were the adolescent "rites of passage" of other times, and to expect kids of today not to be caught up in the culture of their own time is to expect human nature suddenly and miraculously to become something that it is not.

Thus, the influence of peers has a great deal to do with today's drug experimentation. Like it or not, peer pressure often takes precedence over parental influence during the adolescent years. Whereas during childhood the family provides insulation from life's more frightening realities, during the teen-age years the peer group tends to fulfill this protective function. There is a feeling of safety when everyone in the teen-ager's peer group gives approval to a particular kind of behavior.

And we need only to recall the oldest story in the world—Adam and Eve in the Garden of Eden—to be reminded that curiosity—experimentation with the unknown, with the mysterious, with the *forbidden*—is one of man's (and woman's) most basic instincts. Drug experimentation is fueled by curiosity and by a sense of mystery. It simply does no good to tell kids what the drug experience is like if they haven't tried it first-hand.

We have already observed in other sections how teen-agers struggle to become independent and thus find their own identities. Participation in an activity that society has forbidden is a way for teen-agers to assert their independence. In a puff of smoke there is the illusion of instant adulthood.

Teen-agers who feel anger or resentment toward their parents oftentimes take a perverse pleasure in hanging out with a crowd whom the parents disapprove of. This is the adolescent's way of telling the parents, "I can do anything I want to do, and you can't stop me."

Angry parents who try to stop their youngsters from associating with a certain crowd by imposing disciplinary sanctions are almost invariably doomed to failure. The harder parents come down on the kids, the more alienated the kids are likely to become from the parents. In such circumstances, the kids may, in fact, be pushed into the waiting arms of other alienated kids who welcome new recruits as a justification of their own existence. Supported by their peers, it is natural for kids who feel misunderstood at home to experience a new heady feeling of being "outlaws" together—arraigned against their parents and against the society that their parents seem to represent.

The kind of situation described is not uncommon, and sometimes results in children running away from home. Unless care is taken, matters can escalate and create even more serious problems as time goes on. This certainly is a situation to be avoided if at all possible.

But beyond experimentation, beyond peer pressure, beyond feelings of independence and occasional rebelliousness, we must ask what it is that causes some teen-agers to drift deeper and deeper into the morass of either alcoholism or drug use, or both.

One young teen-ager I worked with who was *not* a confirmed drug user but whose parents brought him to me because he was hanging out with a crowd of known heavy drug users characterized his gang peers most accurately and succinctly at one point when he admitted: "They're just losers. Stoned all the time. They don't want to face up to anything."

Experimentation is one thing—and perhaps to be expected—but kids who fall into heavy drug or alcohol use, or both, are troubled kids who essentially are trying to evade life. Drugs are a way of obliterating the constant "down" feelings they experience as a result of a variety of problems that have not been solved. It is true that drugs temporarily do interrupt the monotony of life, and often intensify visual, aural or tactile perception, thus pushing aside the painful present by eliminating the psyche's natural safeguards against failure and danger (that is, guilt, willpower, anxiety). These safeguards and the painful emotions that they cause are replaced by feelings of, "I don't care," or 'Who cares?" As a result, the habitual user tends to avoid all responsibilities, and most importantly, to give up on the necessary search for solutions to life's problems in the face of normal adversity.

Drugs offer the illusory promise of escape from hopelessness by producing temporary peak feelings, or a "high." Drugs lower social anxiety, some drugs producing a "laid-back" feeling of well-being, other drugs providing feelings of invincibility and limitless possibilities of accomplishment in life. (Tuinals, a form of barbituates, are sometimes referred to as "gorilla biscuits" because they make the user feel gargantuan in size, strength or ability.) Suffering from impaired judgment, hardened drug users often demonstrate a clear inability to appreciate the existence of a real potential for committing self-destructive acts. Having escaped death from a close encounter one day, they tend to repeat the same high risk behavior the next day. (This is sometimes referred to as a "nine-lives" syndrome.)

There is certainly no one reason that causes a "down" feeling in teen-agers. Many of the problems that we have discussed in this book, if not solved, potentially could lead to a drug use problem. Boredom, anger, lack of responsibility, failure to communicate with parents, bad schoolwork, lack of friends—all are factors that potentially lay a kid open to the possibility of heavy drug use. The key to blocking a kid's resorting to drugs as a way of life is not so much a matter of trying to explain the danger of drugs or forbidding their use as it is a matter of helping the youngster solve his problems. It is simply true that a healthy youngster who feels good about himself will rarely go beyond mild experimentation and occasional drug use.

Before examining some practical steps that parents can take to help their teen-agers avoid falling in a bad crowd and becoming involved in heavy drug use, let's look at two case histories of two very different kinds of youngsters.

CASE STUDY I—JANE L.

The Complaint

When I opened my office door the first time to greet Jane L. and her mother and father, there were a few seconds when it appeared to me that the two women standing before me were sisters. Mrs. L. was a striking beauty, a former model, with a teen-ager's complexion. Her daughter Jane, though just 16, easily could have passed for a young woman in her middle 20's.

"There's a TV soap commercial here," I thought to myself. But before I could indulge this fantasy further, Mr. L. jumped in with a whole series of complaints. Jane, it seemed, was becoming "uncontrollable." She absolutely refused to come home within curfew hours set by her mother and father, and one recent night she hadn't come home at all. Worst of all, Mrs. L. recently had found marijuana in her daughter's purse, which led to a search through her bureau dresser where a "hashish pipe" turned up.

"She's becoming a drug addict, Doctor," Mr. L. exclaimed. "You can see it in her eyes. She hangs out with an older crowd, and she goes with them to discos without asking our permission. It's okay to have a lust for life, but she's out of control. We're wondering if we ought to be thinking about putting her away in a sanitorium."

Jane's silence in the face of these accusations seemed to confirm her father's suspicions. Before we could get any kind of response from her, however, our time was up, and we made an appointment for Jane to see me next alone.

Without her parents present, Jane told quite a different version of the story than that provided by her father. Yes, she admitted, she had stayed out beyond curfew a couple of times. When she had gotten home, her father had locked her out, telling her through the peep-hole in the door to leave. (Her mother had let her in the house after her father had gone back to bed.)

On the one occasion when she had stayed out all night, Jane had been driving home from a party with her boyfriend when they had had a blowout. Unable to change the flat in the darkness, they had hitch-hiked back to the boyfriend's house where she slept on the floor in the living room.

Jane added: "My father doesn't trust me. There's no point in explaining anything to him. He only tells me I'm lying."

"What about drugs?" I asked her.

"That's a joke," she said. "They think I'm a pot-head because they found a pipe and tiny bit of grass. I hardly ever smoke the stuff, but they're flipping out, driving me crazy."

The facts as both sides described them were the same. But the interpretation was somewhat different.

Background

It was obvious that Jane was no "plain Jane." She was a strikingly attractive and mature-looking young lady. She had a beautiful face, framed by straight black hair, and a voluptuous, well-proportioned figure. Because of her precocious development, Jane did tend to "hang out" with an older crowd. She felt perfectly comfortable with college girls and boys.

In addition to everything else, Jane was a spirited, quick and fiery individual, and at this stage of her life she was fighting hard to establish her own adulthood. Having her own hashish pipe and a small amount of marijuana in her purse was one way of demonstrating to herself and to her friends her independence.

Unfortunately, precisely because of her advanced looks and independent nature, coupled with her young and tender years, her parents were scared to death that she would get over her head in activities that were too much for her. They feared a pregnancy, and they feared she would slip into a world of dissipation and drug use.

What Jane's parents didn't know, and what I came to learn as a result of several sessions alone with her, was that she was a very sensible young lady whose plans in life did *not* call for dissipation and drug use, but on the contrary, she looked forward to going on to college and studying sociology. At the same time, she was sensitive enough (tenderhearted might be even a better term) to contemplate the emotional effect that her going away to college might have on her parents. She actually posed the questions: Would her parents be lonely without her? Would they miss her? Would they forget about her? Would they ever come to appreciate her?

This was no drug addict. This was one special beautiful girl whose parents perhaps loved her very much, but not very wisely. It was imperative, I felt, to get everyone to see a bit more clearly who they were dealing with—*not* because there was a danger that Jane would ever slip into drug addiction, but because the family was creating needlessly hateful scenes that did have the potential for creating wounds that might take many painful years to heal.

Reaching Understanding

Something Mr. L. had said at our very first meeting seemed to pop out at me from my notes as I puzzled over how to help this troubled family overcome so many established misunderstandings. Mr. L. had said: "It's okay to have a lust for life, but she's out of control."

What I wondered was, Did Mr. L. *really* think it was okay to have a lust for life; did he, in fact, recognize the strong positive lust for life that his daughter had? At one of our group family sessions I asked him these very questions.

Not totally surprisingly, Mr. L. admitted that as a young man he had been just as "wild" as his daughter had been. There were many occasions, he said, when he had drunk too much at fraternity parties, and he remembered one "horrible time" when he had gotten sick on frozen daiquiris. "To this day," he said, "I can't stand the taste of a daiquiri."

"But you didn't become an alcoholic," I put in.

"Well, no, of course not," he replied. "I like a drink, but I'm not about to ruin my life."

"Do you think your daughter is somewhat the way you were when you were younger?" I asked him.

"Possibly," he replied.

"Do you think she wants to ruin her life?"

"I don't want to ruin my life, Dad!" Jane exclaimed suddenly with great passion. "I'm going to do things with my life! I'm going to college next year! I can't wait to get into it!"

Despite my customary professional detachment, there was a moment when I felt like reaching out and hugging her. I was glad to see that Mrs. L. felt no similar need to remain detached. She took her daughter's hand in her own. Mr. L. simply looked down. From the expression on his partially hidden face, it was obvious that he had gotten the message, too.

Creative Synthesis

Reassured somewhat by the basic serious outlook and positive intentions of their daughter, Mr. and Mrs. L. in the weeks that followed made a point of allowing certain new concessions to Jane that they had never allowed before. On one occasion, they allowed her to spend a week-end out of town with a girlfriend who was in college. When there were no catastrophic results, Mrs. L. reported that she was both surprised and relieved.

I was relieved, too, but I wasn't surprised.

Jane, on the other hand, was ecstatic—not about any new liberties given to her, but about the atmosphere in the home.

"Both of my parents' attitude is so much better," she told me. "Like, they treat me like an adult all of a sudden. It makes me *feel* adult, and I don't have to prove anything to anybody."

In the few remaining sessions that I had with Jane she boasted about having learned to control her temper with her father. "He's trying," she said. "He really is a good guy."

A few months later, after we had discontinued therapy, Jane called to tell me that she had been accepted into the college of her choice, and was going to fly to the campus with her mother the following week-end. She just had to tell me that her grades had suddenly picked up, and she had written a story in English class that was accepted by the school literary publication. The theme: self-discovery.

What should be emphasized in connection with this case history is that during the last few sessions with Jane, and during the later phone conversation with her the matter of drugs was never even mentioned. The whole subject had become irrelevant to the real development that was going on with her. And this was the case of a young lady whose father had wanted to incarcerate her in a sanitorium for drug addicts.

CASE HISTORY II—PETER R.

The Complaint

When 16-year-old Peter R. and his mother and father came to their first visit in my office, Peter appeared to be in deep trouble, and the direction he was moving in was pointing further down. The problems he was facing were not just the figment of her parents' imagination, either. He was flunking three courses in his sophomore year in high school, and in conference with his parents his teachers complained that he seemed totally uninterested in his classes, that most of the time he failed to do homework assignments, and that he *didn't even get started* on term papers. Instead of listening in class, apparently he would spend much of his time there drawing caricatures of the teachers (some of which at a later time he showed me, and they were quite good). In several instances, he had been verbally abusive to his history teacher, and also to several of his fellow students in class. He absolutely refused to participate in any kind of sports activity, and although sports participation was not a school requirement, the school was very proud of its reputation for producing some outstanding county athletes; teen-agers who did not participate tended to be somewhat frowned upon.

That was just the start. Earlier in the year, during the first week of school, Peter had been caught smoking marijuana with another boy in the lavatory, and had been suspended for a week. At about the same time, his mother had found a hashish pipe under his pillow and an ounce of marijuana in the top drawer of his dresser. Meanwhile, he was growing marijuana in a flower pot on his windowsill, and when it was discovered, he tried to maintain that it was a *carrot* plant.

What finally aroused his family to bring him to see me was an incident involving the police. Peter had been "hanging out" with an older crowd of high school drop-outs. The favorite hangout place of this particular crowd was the town public park. The town council had recently taken note of their presence by passing a law against public drinking. One of the older kids had given Peter a beer, which Peter had only started to drink when the police jumped out of the bushes and arrested the two of them. Spread eagled against a tree, Peter was searched, and the police found *another* hashish pipe with a small amount of marijuana in the bowl. This was in April, and his court case (as a juvenile offender) was due to come up in early June.

Indeed, this was no misunderstood Jane L. Here

was a kid who was on the verge, as his father put it, of "going down the tube."

Background

Although Peter's parents were very concerned about their son, at the same time they were convinced that he was a "good boy" and were anxious to do whatever was necessary to "get him on the right track."

Both Mr. and Mrs. R. were bright, and extremely creative, and saw themselves as somewhat outside of the mainstream life of the small town they had moved to from New York 17 years ago, before Peter was even born. Both Mr. and Mrs. R. had been "pretty far out" radicals during the 1960's, and, in fact, had met at a training seminar on non-violent protest against the Vietnam war. They both still held political opinions quite far to the left. Mr. R. had published a novel ten years before describing what life in the '60's had been like for young idealistic radicals. (The book was not a great success, but one couldn't help but get the impression on reading it that Mr. R.'s life as a young radical had been an experience he did not regret.) Marriage and the birth of Peter and the birth of a daughter, Gigi—Peter's 13-year-old sister—had mellowed both parents. Mr. R. now conducted a successful public relations business employing two other people, working out of offices attached to the R. house. Mrs. R. was an accomplished painter with a reputation of sorts, and in her studio in back of their house produced impressive oils, some of which were owned by several collectors and museums.

Thus, Peter's "outsider" behavior pattern did not

particularly concern Mr. and Mrs. R. In fact, up until his problem with drugs, they had been more or less proud of him for his independent spirit.

Now, however, with Peter's recent problems, the parents were not so sure but what they had made, in the words of Mrs. R., "a terrible mistake."

"We brought Peter up to think for himself, and to be skeptical of a lot of the conventional teen-age junk that exists in the world," Mrs. R. said, "but he seems to be left with just the skepticism and nothing positive to grab onto."

Peter himself seemed genuinely confused about his life and where and how he fitted into it. A handsome boy, his reluctance to participate in organized sports was certainly not the result of any athletic ability. One of the few things he enjoyed was lifting weights, and he was as strong as any of the "jocks" on the football team whom he held somewhat in contempt.

Among the group of outsiders that he was hanging out with, he was looked up to not only for his physical strength but for his "ideas," most of which had to do with matters, such as loyalty to one's friends, the broadening of one's horizons, travel and "adventure."

As far as his various transgressions were concerned, Peter felt no particular guilt or sorrow. Privately he told me that he felt his parents "worried too much," and that if they would get off his "case," he would be all right. He made no apologies for the pleasure he got from "mellowing out" occasionally while he listened to music (his favorite music being the hard rock variety, what else?), but that he didn't really think of himself as a "pothead." It had been "dumb" getting caught smoking in the school lavatory, he felt, and it had been "a bad break" getting caught with a beer ("and the dope") in the town park.

As far as school was concerned, he hated math, couldn't see any reason for studying French, and had utmost contempt for his history teacher (the one he had been abusive to), whom he described as a "wimp." Peter *did* like his art teacher, and was managing to get a B+ in his art course.

It took a bit of time to win Peter's confidence sufficiently so that he would talk about himself. When he did finally open up to me, what emerged was a picture of him that matched the one I had already begun to form.

Reaching Understanding

What seemed clear to me was that Peter was a young man with the very same kind of romantic idealistic nature that his parents had had 20 years before, the difference being that in the present era he had been unable to find a satisfactory outlet for his feelings. The few walkathons that Mr. and Mrs. R. had participated in during recent times on behalf of the Nuclear Freeze Movement, Peter would have nothing to do with. (It was too closely identified in his mind with his parents and other "old people.")

As a result, Peter, by his own admission, was bored to death. His particular interests, which were introspective rather than of a boisterous socializing nature, were not being met either by his school, or by the majority of kids in the school. Most significantly, he was not so much enamored of the drug-taking crowd as he was disaffected from everyone else. In short, he was looking for alternatives to the conventional type of life that the town seemed to offer. Because he couldn't find anything at this stage of his life that satisfied him, he had drifted toward other disaffected kids, the drug-taking crowd.

What Peter needed, it seemed to me, was an outlet for his idealism and sensitivity that would be positive, drawing away from the negative influence of others in the drug crowd. He also needed to explore further his artistic talents.

Creative Synthesis

Without so much as even mentioning the word drugs, Peter and his parents and I discussed what he would like most to do during the upcoming school summer vacation. I was glad to see that Peter was an enthusiastic participant in this discussion.

The first thing that he had to put behind him was 39 hours of community service that he had been sentenced to by the court in early June for his recent drug bust.* His servitude involved digging a town drainage ditch with a road crew, which to Peter seemed almost like a *reward* rather than a punishment. With his shirt off in the hot June sun, he stood side by side with the other construction workers and swung his pick. When his time was up, his father told me that the construction crew put down their tools and applauded as Mr. R. waited at the curbside with the car.

One of the things Peter liked to do with some of the more adventurous members of his crowd was to climb local cliffs. Mr. R. picked up on this, and asked

---

*As a juvenile offender, he would have no police record if the 39 hours of community service were performed satisfactorily.

Peter if he would like to participate in a Colorado Outward Bound rock climbing expedition.

"Ye-e-e-a-a-h!" Peter said.

Peter spent one month in Colorado in a rigorous mountain climbing Outward Bound program (paying the tuition from his own savings; his father paid for his round-trip plane fare). In a report that his guide filed one month later, Peter was described as having made "an outstanding contribution" to the group, having shown consideration in helping some of the physically weaker members of the group to surmount difficult obstacles and "displaying genuine leadership abilities."

With his successful participation in two activities that challenged his physical abilities, Peter already was exhibiting a new spring in his step and an occasional hint of a winning smile.

Following Peter's return from Colorado, the family took their annual three-week vacation to Cape Cod where Mrs. R. customarily did a great deal of painting every year. Mr. and Mrs. R. were able to enroll Peter in an art program in Provincetown, and it was here that he truly found himself. The other art students were mostly in their 20's, and having already struggled through their teen-age confusions, including drug experimentation, were now dedicated artists, romantic idealists themselves, somewhat outside the mainstream of conventional society, but very much in love with life itself and full of future plans. With these young people as role models, it suddenly dawned on Peter that his independence from the mainstream life of his hometown was not "weird," that he could be different without necessarily identifying himself with society's drug drop-outs.

Peter R.'s parents played a very low-key but critical role in guiding their son into positive paths during that turning-point summer. It was a time when Peter grew up a lot. He went back to school that fall, and his days as a heavy "doper" were over. He managed to find a few friends (including one girl who was talented artistically) who shared some of his own ideas. In time, without having to submit to the athletic and other social demands of the majority group, Peter and his circle actually managed to win the respect of other of their classmates.

Once in a while Peter would run across his old drug crowd whose members were still swigging beers out of paper bags and toking on joints. He told me he felt sorry for the old group. "They're all right," he said, "but they're not going anywhere, and they know it." When he would encounter them, in keeping with his idealistic notions of loyalty, he never snubbed them; he would stop and talk with them, joking and laughing. But he always declined their offers to smoke a joint or have a beer.

There was no more need for therapy. Peter had had a close call. At one of our last sessions, he told me he would still smoke a joint now and then, and his parents seemed to know it, and it didn't bother them. As far as his classroom work was concerned, having managed to squeak through math the previous June (with a D), he was repeating his year in French. Though he still did not like the subject, he felt now that he could get through it.

"I need the credit to get into a good art school," he said.

Practical Steps

The two case histories that we have just seen illustrate opposite ends of the teen-age drug spectrum today. One child, Jane L., was involved in drugs only to the slightest extent in an experimental way. The other youngster, Peter R., may have been on the brink of tumbling into a heavy drug habit. In both instances, sensible preventive action by the parents provided valuable help in enabling these teen-agers to pass through difficult periods.

I. Don't go "crazy"

If and when it becomes clearly apparent that your teen-ager is using, or has used, some form of drugs or alcohol, don't panic. Recognize that in today's world the child who does not at least experiment one or two times with drugs is a rare exception. Your job as a sensible concerned parent is not to go "crazy" with a lot of unfounded assumptions and accusations, but to try, first of all, to *determine the extent of drug use* by your child, and then act accordingly.

II. What is behind your child's use of drugs?

Is your child merely dipping experimentally into the "mystique" of drugs. Is your child merely trying to be "one of the gang" and going along one or two times as a result of peer pressure? Is your child trying to "act grown up" by showing you and himself/herself that he/she can be "real bad" in the contemporary world? Jane L. was such a child.

Or is your child in some kind of deeper trouble? Are you able to link up your teen-ager's use of drugs with other adolescent problems, many of which we deal with in this book?

Before you can react in a helpful and positive way, it is important to *get to the bottom of what is behind the drug taking.*.

The case of Peter R., for example, was a typical instance of a child whose life was *boring*, and consequently unhappy. Peter needed to find suitable outlets for his physical strength and for his somewhat individualistic notions.

If you listen to what your teen-ager has to say, you may be able to lead him or her into activities that will be sufficiently interesting to turn him or her away from heavy drug use. A *delicate touch* is critical here. The object is *not* to suggest to your kid such-and-such an activity or interest as an alternative to drug taking; more to the point, if the child takes strongly to a new activity or interest, the interest in drugs oftentimes will diminish by itself.

III. Be curious, but don't jump down your kid's throat.

If you suspect that your child is using drugs, confronting him/her in a hostile manner and making threats usually does very little good. My advice is to talk with your youngster about the subject of drugs in a non-hostile way. Let your kid know that you are aware of peer pressures today; that you are aware of the curiosity that teen-agers inevitably must have about drugs; that your main concern is not whether or not your youngster has tried drugs, but more with the consequences of heavy drug use.

Try to find out your child's own feelings about the use of drugs. If your teen-ager feels he can talk with you in a reasonably honest way about drug use, you have removed instantly one of the most common reasons for children to use drugs—to shock their parents into a recognition that they are growing up.

IV. How to help your teen-ager cope with peer pressure

Peer influences, as we have seen, are extremely powerful during adolescence. To turn down the offer of drugs from one's peers is a formidable challenge, even for the secure and self-assured teen-ager. If you should be fortunate enough to have a teen-ager who seeks your advice on such matters, tell the child that one is no less of a person—and, in fact, is *more* of a person—by having the courage to decline the offer of drugs. It takes a big person to dissent from the crowd. A child who declines the offer of drugs without judging those who have offered them does *not* risk losing the friendship of anyone whose friendship counts. Tell your children this.

V. A change of context sometimes helps

Parents whose children are involved with a bad crowd where drug use is prevalent frequently ask me if they should pull their children out of a particular school environment, and transfer them to another. My answer to the question is that change in environment does not necessarily always prove helpful. After all, drug users and drugs are everywhere, and if a child is determined to hang out with particular kinds of kids, he will find them no matter where he goes. On the other hand, a change in environment *sometimes* can be helpful, particularly if the teen-ager himself suggests it, and has indicated a strong desire to make a fresh start. If the child himself thinks he can do better in another context—

partly because of current negative peer influences that he wants to avoid, and perhaps also because of a bad reputation with present school authorities that may be almost irreversible—a change might be indicated. The child should be made to understand, however, that a change will create some new problems, too, such as the matter of making new friends, accommodating to a new situation, following new rules.

Getting Peter R. out of town during the summer vacation certainly had a salutary effect in that particular situation. Summertime is a good time to make a change, because it is a natural time to move around. Moreover, the child who is moved into a new environment in the summer is not made to feel like a quitter or a failure, as sometimes can happen if a change in schools is made in the middle of a term.

VI. Point out the dangers of drug use

Because children will never be as conscious of dangers as their parents, it behooves every parent to alert their teen-agers to the harmful consequences of heavy drug use. This does not mean that you should throw at your kid every latest medical bulletin that appears in the news media on the "damaging effects of drugs on the brain," or whatever. I personally think that to whatever extent such reports are true they have no effect on teenagers at all. In fact, speaking of them merely serves to turn teen-agers off.

I do believe, however, that many teen-agers who experiment with drugs are to some extent conscious of the high risk of automobile fatalities as a result of drug use. (What city or town in America doesn't have the example of at least one high school kid who has been lost in a drug or alcohol related automobile accident?) It is appropriate to raise this matter with teen-agers, and to warn them against mixing drug use with vehicular use.

And, of course, there are legal consequences of drug use, as Peter R. found out. It is entirely appropriate, I believe, for parents to remind their teen-agers that "controlled substances" are illegal, and that the consequences for those caught using them can be serious. Particularly serious are drug arrests in connection with automobile accidents. The message is: Beware, kids. You can hurt yourself; you can hurt someone else; you can ruin a lot of lives.

VII. Are you a heavy drug user yourself?

Did you think you were going to get off the hook without a word about your own use of drugs? Do you smoke an occasional joint now and then? Do you snort cocaine? Do you smoke *cigarettes*? Are you a heavy drinker?

These are all drugs. And if you are a heavy cigarette smoker, or have a *daily routine* of drinking a couple of martinis before dinner—enough to get a bit high every day—you are setting an example of drug use for your children.

I am not a teetotaller. I like a cocktail now and then. I like a glass of wine with dinner; I think wine enhances the flavor of food. I commend its use, in fact, to my readers. I am strongly opposed, however, to heavy drinking—for a lot of reasons. For the purposes of this book, I oppose it because it sets a bad drug example for teen-age kids.

I am even more adamant in my bias against cigarette smoking. Anyone who does not think that cigarette smoking is an addiction has never tried to "kick the habit." Again, it is not within the purview of this book to talk of the dangers of cigarette smoking. But *the dangers are real*. And cigarettes are a *drug*. To those who are heavy drinkers or who smoke cigarettes, I simply say that you are setting a bad example for your kids.

I will add this: Those of you who have been addicted and succeed in *giving up* smoking are setting a wonderful example to your teen-age kids. They know from what they have learned as little children that cigarette smoking is harmful. Yes, they really have absorbed that lesson. If they see you struggling to give up your habit, and succeeding, they will be left with an indelible positive example that will serve them well all through their difficult teen-age years. It is the best incentive I know of for adults to give up smoking cigarettes. And it is the most valuable gift you could possibly offer to your child.

Problem #9

~~~~~~

"What About My Kid and Sex?"

Next to the weather, there is no subject known to man more talked about than sex. Sex flourishes in the hogans and hovels of downtrodden masses, as well in the palaces of kings and queens. Sex has been alternately praised or blamed for every vice, calamity, victory, triumph, defeat, conquest, tragedy, and bitter consequence known to man. Songs are written about it, poems are written about it, *laws* are written about it. It just seems as though we "can't help luvin' dat man" or woman. Prospects for its continuance, regardless of whatever else continues or ceases to continue, are very good. Sex, love it or hate it, is here to stay.

Human sexuality exists in infinite varieties and in all age groups, depending upon individual cases.

There are octogenarians and nonagenarians who engage in an active sex life. From the earliest years, infant boys and girls engage in a kind of pleasurable sexual activity by examining the various parts of their own bodies. Spurred initially by curiosity and the instinct to explore, children quickly learn that tactile contact with certain parts of their bodies produces sensual pleasure. By the age of four it is common for boys and girls to "play doctor." Boys of the same age will sometimes play sexually with other boys of the same age, and the same is true for girls, and there seems to be no correlation between this kind of activity and adult homosexuality.

True sexuality, however, with its full potential for pleasure as well as for serious consequences, first manifests itself in the teen-age years.* It is during this period that an activity that has been primarily experimental, though pleasurable, becomes a physiological drive. Teen-agers become "hot to trot."

It is during the teen-age years that the human biological alarm clock first signals that it is time to replenish the species. That clock may ring for another 30, 40, 50 or however many years, but the batteries will never be stronger than they are at the start. Teen-agers, like adults, experience this signal as bodily tension, otherwise known as "horniness." Like hunger, sexual arousal begs for gratification to ease the tension. Only by resorting to some purposeful behavior (sexual intercourse, or masturbation), or the unconscious equivalent (nocturnal

---

*Actually, with the improvement in nutrition levels in industrialized nations of the world, girls are menstruating at earlier and earlier ages, even *before* the onset of the teens. Some girls are able to bear children—and *do*—at an age when they themselves are pre-adolescent children, as young as 12, or even under.

emission), does the tension subside. Until the next time.

This sexual tension insinuates itself deeply into the lives of teen-agers, and *cannot be denied*. It results in teen-agers' first efforts at dating and experimenting with adult sexuality. The major problem with this natural activity is that in our culture our biology is somewhat ahead of our ability to take on the consequences of "going all the way." In other cultures—particularly where life conditions are hard and longevity is short—it may be desirable to breed a new generation at the earliest possible moment. In some cultures the family, or tribe, takes on the responsibility for the young mother and her babe until such time as the babe arrives at an age when it can contribute to the general good. In our society, a female, depending on her social expectations, in most instances is not ready to take on responsibility for an offspring until she has a more or less dependable mate and/or an education or job (with pregnancy insurance, leave of absence guarantees, etc.)

Thus, in our society as soon as teen-agers reach the dating age parents cannot help but be concerned about the possibility of an unwanted pregnancy. It only takes one time for a girl to become pregnant, and there is no reason why that one time should not be the *first* time, particularly because the first time is when a girl may be most vulnerable. When she is least experienced about her own body, and least experienced in how to protect it from impregnation, she is most likely to conceive.

But an unwanted pregnancy is not the only possible bitter consequence of teen-age sexuality. Parents have other concerns, too—concerns having to do with such things as rules and limits on dating (particularly when dating is connected with riding in automobiles); promiscuity and a resultant bad reputation; and its opposite, a lack of interest in members of the opposite sex (and, therefore, the possibility of a homosexual tendency); the influence of pornography and associated masturbation; the pressure of peers to involve a teen-ager in sexual activities that he or she may not be ready for; the danger of venereal disease.

These are just a few of the concerns that parents of teen-agers have. Because each generation adheres to different standards from the preceding generation, parents are frequently at a disadvantage in knowing how to deal with the teen-age sexual behavior of their children.

Teen-age Sexuality in Today's World

Teen-agers, like everyone else, do not live in an isolation booth. With all of their sexual urges, obsessions, longings and compulsions, they live in the real world of today, and in case anybody is not aware, the western world has gone through a so-called sexual revolution since the 1960's. (The sexual revolution probably got its start back in the days of World War II, but it really picked up steam in the decades that followed.)

Although the dust has settled slightly on the nuttier antics of the 60's when bra burning, public nudity, promiscuity and even group sex were somewhat the fad, still, changes in sexual practices, including a greater freedom to participate in premarital and non-marital sex, are here to stay. At least, they are here to stay for a while, until someone comes along and convinces the next generation that the highest form of sexuality is *no*-sex, or trapeze sex, or zero gravity sex, or whatever other kind of sex the human imagination can come up with.

My own feeling is that, by and large, the sexual revolution of recent times, in general, has had some positive effects on human attitudes. For one thing, the sexual revolution has resulted in the acknowledgment, perhaps for the first time in human history, that women have the same sexual rights as men—that is, sex is an activity to be enjoyed by *both* partners, and not just by men. In effect, the acceptance of this notion liberated women from a kind of servitude that implied that their own feelings and desires were secondary to those of men. (The social implications of this acknowledged equality, incidentally, go far beyond the limits of sexual activity alone.)

Moreover, the sexual revolution has resulted in a wider acceptance of sexual intercourse as a possibility outside of the institution of marriage. I myself am married, and I like marriage, but I recognize the right of others to have sex outside of marriage, and I know people who live together in a sexual relationship who are not married. This is fairly common today.

In short, the sexual revolution has resulted in more of a tendency to *allow consenting adults to do what they want to do, as long as they don't hurt anyone, including themselves*—in the vernacular, "different strokes for different folks." And, by and large, I think this is a positive development.

On the other hand, there is no doubt that the liberalization of sex attitudes has decimated some of our *moral* positions having to do with sexual relationships and associated matters, such things as virtue and virginity, birth control, and abortion. To appreciate the wide schism that has taken place in American society with regard to these subjects, all you have to do is pick up any morning newspaper or watch television. There you will find people on both sides of the issues debating passionately. Indeed, some groups and individuals have gone beyond debating, and have even resorted to violence, in the case of abortion clinics, to make their point.

There is no doubt but what the loosening of sexual moral sanctions has resulted in a much more open and explicit depiction of sexual attitudes and practices in the communications and entertainment media. A generation ago married couples in movies could be shown sleeping in the same room together only if they were in twin beds. Now we can observe them as closely as if we were medical students crowded around an operating table while they writhe and cavort in the nude and perform awesome drill routines of sexual acrobatics.

The advertising industry has always known that a pretty girl is a good way to draw attention to a product. But whereas at one time the Morton Salt girl stood in a raincoat and poured her salt, today the media hucksters beckon and urge millions of viewers to join in a more glamorous lifestyle through the depiction of legions of scantily clad teenagers cavorting on beaches, drinking sodas and beer, eating, vacationing, displaying watches, exercising, driving automobiles, reading books, washing dishes and operating computers. These just for starters.

In a similar but even more blatantly pornographic manner, the new rock video craze exploits sexual imagery, oftentimes in combination with violent behavior (sado-masochism). The aim seems to be for rock performers to draw attention to themselves by means of ever escalating no-holds-barred appeals to the nihilistic side of contemporary visions of the world.

Much of this advertising and rock video depiction of sexuality today is at variance with the *human content* behind sexual relationships, and presents a very distorted picture to teen-agers at a time when they are attempting to develop their initial attitudes about sex. Teen-agers who are searching for outlets to their new explosive sexual urges are being provided with images of behavior that are, in fact, in conflict with their most basic needs as human beings.

What most healthy adults ultimately learn is that sexual activity is most rewarding when it is part of a mutually admiring and affectionate human relationship; when it is non-exploitative (that is, when it does not serve the interests of one partner at the expense of another); when it is caring and respectful. Images that portray sexuality as ego enchancement, or, worse, as anger or hate gratification, do a disservice to teen-agers, and go a long way toward contributing to confusion about the very nature of sex.

What Parents Want to Know About Teen-Age Sexual Behavior

Some adults may feel that it is not appropriate for people of any age to have sexual intercourse outside of marriage. Others may condone the idea of pre-marital sex, but not for teen-agers. And still others may feel that sexual intercourse is appropriate for teen-agers who are ready for it.

I respect all of these points of view, but from my experience I would say that in today's world it really doesn't matter an awful lot what adults approve of or disapprove of. Some teen-agers will not indulge in sexual intercourse, and others will—regardless of what their parents want. Consequently, without necessarily advocating sexual intercourse for teen-agers, I think that parents *should be prepared for the possibility*, even likelihood, of its occurring.

The question for parents today, it seems to me, is not whether or not they should permit their teen-ager to have sexual relations, but, rather, how best to deal with the eventuality of teen-age sexual intercourse, if it should occur. This approach means parents can at least provide guidance and help to their children so that there are no harmful effects from their experiences.

At What Age Is Sexual Intercourse Appropriate?

"Doctor, I know my daughter wants to sleep with her boyfriend. But do you think she is old enough?"

This is a question that I am asked very often by parents. And I have to say that there is no stock answer. Some children—both boys and girls—are physiologically and psychologically prepared for sex at very early ages, and others are not ready until much later. (Some people *never* reach sufficient psychological maturity to handle a sexual relationship.)

As I have indicated, a sexual relationship should

be based first of all on feelings of *human affection between two people*. It should be *non-exploitative*; that is, not serving the interests of one partner at the expense of the other. And it should be *mutually caring and respectful*. To this, I would add—particularly in the case of teen-agers—that both loving partners should have *sufficient maturity* to understand that there are *consequences connected with sexual intercourse*. A pregnancy could easily develop if proper precautions of one kind or another are not taken.

What do I mean by "human affection that is non-exploitative and mutually caring and respectful"?

The vast majority of teen-age romances can be classified as "puppy love." That is, two kids who are "hot to trot" share a transient common interest in one thing or another—perhaps a rock group, a study program, a leisure time activity, notions of ideal physical beauty, whatever, it doesn't matter. The opinions and interests of both kids almost invariably will change in a short period of time, almost as quickly as there occurs a change in the direction of the wind. And just as quickly, the two kids will lose interest in one another, though not without a certain amount of sadness. That's "puppy love."

This may surprise readers, but regardless of its fleeting nature, I do believe that *"puppy love" is a valid form of human affection that should be taken seriously by parents*. It is taken *terribly seriously* by the teen-agers who are smitten. Although it most likely will pass, while it exists, teen-agers may be drawn together irresistibly by sexual passion. If the kids feel genuine affection for each other, they may very well be ready psychologically for sexual intercourse.

On the other hand, to be avoided at all cost is the "exploitative relationship" in which one partner's sexual interests are served at the expense of the other's. What, precisely, do I mean by this? I mean a situation in which one partner who is not ready for a sexual involvement, or who is tentative about it, is *pressured* to participate by the other partner. I am talking about the partner who says, "If you really love, me, you'll go all the way." I'm talking about partners who want a sexual encounter so as to be able to brag to friends, or to prove something to themselves.

Teen-age kids who allow themselves to be talked into doing something that basically they do not want to do, or that they are not sure whether or not they want to do—regardless of the reason for their reluctance, moral or otherwise—can be hurt psychologically by "giving in." It is, in fact, submitting to a kind of rape; it oftentimes is a violation of their own deep-rooted convictions. Observant parents who spot in advance a potential teen-age sexual relationship that is unequal will do well to exert whatever influence they can to discourage it.

Quite aside from being pressured, sexual intercourse by some sensitive teen-agers who have not yet quite come to terms with the idea can lead to post-coital guilt feelings that can be deeply disturbing to them, and interfere with their normal day-to-day functioning. Sexual intercourse by teen-agers is *not* just a matter of "doing it." It has emotional consequences, and some sensitive teen-ager find that it gets them into emotional depths over their heads. Guilt feelings are just one of the possibly negative post-coital reactions. If there is a question about the maturity of a child and his or her readiness to take on the emotional baggage of a sexual relationship, then it would be wise to encourage the child, if possible, to hold off for a while.

For many sensitive young people (not to mention some adults, too) sexual intercourse implies a commitment and an overriding sense of responsibility to the other person. Although adults usually learn how to organize these feelings into manageable proportions (oftentimes by developing a very selectively discriminating approach in sexual matters), teen-agers, on the other hand sometimes find themselves overwhelmed by a sense of responsibility. Should the teen-ager date other people while having sex with a certain partner? This is a difficult question to answer for a sensitive teenager whose psychic identity is still unformed. In such a circumstance, a common scenario that is not a happy one is for a teen-ager (of either sex) to sustain a commitment that he/she no longer feels, and thus proceed into an unwanted marriage that very likely will only end in divorce a year or two or three later.

One 17-year old girl told me that she gave up going out with all of her friends (both male and female) and stayed home week-end nights for four months because her boyfriend worked during week-end night hours and she felt that if she enjoyed herself in any way it would be an act of disloyalty. (She came to me for counseling when she discovered that her boyfriend was "cheating" on her with one of her girlfriends from the neighborhood).

Other Situations When Sexual Intercourse Should Be Discouraged

As we have noted many times in the course of this book, the teen-age years are a time of rebellion, a time of establishing a new independence, a time of confusion and anger, a time of laxity in taking on adult responsibilities, a time of seeking to be popular.

Sometimes a teen-ager will use sex as a way of acting out one or more of these needs. A daughter, for instance, who is angry at her parents and wants to establish her own adult independence might very well become involved in a sexual relationship in the expectation that it will at the same time hurt her parents while providing her with a new sense of independence from them.

A boy who seeks popularity among his peers by establishing a reputation as a macho lover may very well go about attempting to seduce as many girls as possible. Implicit in such behavior, of course, is the so-called "double-standard" whereby we wink at boys who make out with girls, and disapprove of girls who are "easy." It is sad that society condemns promiscuous girls as bad or as "sluts" while there persists a tendency to admire boys who can get as much sex as they can. ("Get much lately?" is not so much a question as it is an encouragement for boys to go out and seduce girls.) The truth is, however, that compulsive "Don Juan" behavior is as much of a desperate effort on the part of boys to build up self-esteem through an appeal to vulgar popularity as it can be a desperate attempt on the part of promiscuous girls to be loved, or to satisfy through a momentary fantasy the need to be cared for.

Parents whose children seem headed into this kind of non-loving sexual involvement will do well to take a closer look at what is behind such behavior. Perhaps some words of understanding or, if needed, reassurance will make a difference, and head off or alter a sexual involvement that can only create more problems than it will solve. It is to no girl's advantage to develop a bad reputation. A girl who persists in pursuing sexual behavior that is damaging to her own reputation (regardless of how "unfair" the double standard may be) is operating out of motives* that have very little to do with sex as a pleasurable experience.

What About the Danger of Pregnancy?

What parents of a teen-age girl haven't wrestled with a nightmare fantasy such as the following?: Their 14-year-old daughter is dating a "nice" boy, and is "crazy" about him. They are together whenever they have the opportunity. After a time, the daughter starts complaining about fatigue and frequent nausea, particularly nausea in the morning. Yes, she is pregnant, and knows it, and bursts into tears in the presence of her mother and father, crying: "I want to keep my baby! Don't try to change my mind!"

---

*Persistent reckless sexual promiscuity can be pathonomic of a serious personality defect, usually associated with deep insecurity feelings, low self esteem, no lasting sense of self importance. In such instances, professional therapeutic attention may be warranted.

As sad as that scenario might be, consider this one (if you haven't already): The same girl is going out with the same boy, but after six weeks they "break up," and again, the girl discovers she is pregnant. She is afraid to tell her parents for fear of their angry reaction. Feeling abandoned, helpless, hopeless, alone and desperate, she chooses to run away from home. The scenario here has a multiple choice ending: She could try to abort herself; maybe, because she is filled with feelings of unworthiness and self-loathing, she could get in with a bad crowd and take up drugs; or, in an act of final desperation, she might conceivably attempt suicide. Or all three.

A tragedy, but one that is as common as what we see daily on television on the six o'clock news.

A teen-age pregnancy means the end of childhood. Whatever plans the girl, or implicated boy, may have had, an unexpected pregnancy introduces a drastic change of course. Thus, good advice, I think, is for parents to sit down with their children *prior* to a pregnancy—and that usually means prior to sexual intercourse—for a frank discussion of how to avoid becoming pregnant.

Discussing with your child the dangers of pregnancy and the various ways of preventing a pregnancy does *not* necessarily mean that you are condoning sexual intercourse by your teen-ager. If you feel that your child is not ready for a full sexual relationship, you can tell your child this. It may even surprise you to find out that your child respects your opinion, and has been just waiting for you to make it known. On the other hand, if your child is determined to have a sexual relationship, regardless of your approval or disapproval, it is far better that the child should be advised on how to take steps to avoid a pregnancy than to simply go ahead willy-nilly without precaution.

If it should so happen that your daughter were to become one of the close to 700,000 unwed females who become pregnant each year in the United States,* whether you approve or not, you will be well advised to support your daughter to the fullest extent possible. You may disapprove of the pregnancy, but you must also remember, that you *love your daughter.* Your child will need you now, as never before, and if you were to turn on her and reject her, in her present state you make her that much more susceptible to taking a possibly destructive course of action.

Finally, with regard to this matter of taking precautionary steps to avoid a pregnancy, the *boy* shares responsibility, too. If your sexually active teen-ager is a boy, he should be advised to take precautions against getting the girl pregnant. If there is a pregnancy, he should understand that he has a moral responsibility to stand by the girl.

What About Dating?

As much as parents are concerned about the possibility of a pregnancy, they are probably even more concerned about the harm that can occur to their children while they are taking part in the rites of

---

*The number and rate of births to unmarried teen-agers, both blacks and whites, have been increasing, having reached close to 700,000 in 1980. The biggest increase has been in the District of Columbia, where 88 per cent of all teen-age mothers in 1982 were unwed. The overall national unmarried birthrate now exceeds 20 percent.—*N.Y. Times,* Oct. 20, 1985.

dating. Better to have a pregnant daughter, or a son implicated in a pregnancy, than to have a child killed in an automobile accident, or drowned at a beach party, or rendered permanently comotose from a drug/alcohol overdose.

Once upon a time teen-agers courted under the watchful eye of chaperones. In some cultures this is still the practice. Obviously, it is not the practice in our culture today. You cannot be there to watch over your child.

What you can do, however—and what you *should* do—is establish certain "dating rules of behavior." We have discussed in other sections how to go about setting up mutually agreed upon rules for your teen-agers. By keeping in mind current peer behavior and reaching a "creative synthesis" with your child, you should be able to establish certain reasonable guidelines.

If your child is going somewhere in an automobile, he/she should understand that drinking/drugs and driving don't mix. Believe me, your kid knows this already. A gentle reminder may elicit the customary, "I know, Mom!" But it's worth hearing your child exclaim it one more time just to know that you have put out the good word—again. Particularly if your kid is driving *your car* to a party (or rock concert) where drugs and/or alcohol will be available, you have the right (and obligation) to lay down a strict injunction against any drug or alcohol participation whatsoever—*on pain, at the very least, of being denied use of the car again.* Aside from the fact that your child could be hurt or killed in an automobile accident, if your child were to be driving under the influence and an accident should occur in which *other people*—either passengers in the car, or in another car, or pedestrians—were hurt, or killed, your child would be in deep legal trouble.

If your child is going in someone else's car to a gathering where drugs or alcohol will be available, you should instruct your child *not to ride with anyone who has been drinking or taking drugs*. Make it clear to them that they should *get out of the car, and ride with somebody else. Call one of the hot-line numbers that have been established in many communities (often run by teen-agers) and get a safe ride home with a sober driver.* If your kid's date is drunk and driving, your kid will be doing the date a service by not letting him/her drive. Maybe it will take some courage on the part of your child to go against peer pressure in the excitement of the moment, but the next day, sober—and safe—friends will be grateful. Tell your child this—and perhaps save a life.

Find out where your child is going, what kind of activity is anticipated, and what time the child can be expected home. *Negotiate* the curfew hour. Obviously, a prom calls for a later curfew than a Saturday night movie. Be flexible, but once the curfew has been set, let your child know that you expect compliance. (You can allow a half hour leeway.) Let your child know that if a problem arises (such as a flat tire, or whatever) to *call home*. A late night call home in an emergency is preferable to no call. Your child should understand that you will not be angered by a late night call; on the contrary, you will welcome it, if it is necessary, and you will do whatever is called for to help your child in the particular situation.

It's not a bad idea to meet the youngster whom your teen-ager is going out with. If a boy is calling on your daughter with a car, it won't hurt the boy to know that his date has parents who love her and expect her to be treated with respect and consideration. If your son is dating a girl, particularly if he is seeing her on a regular basis, he shouldn't have any objection to bringing her around to meet you. Seeing the girl whom your son is dating, incidentally, will give you added insight into your son.

Sometimes it is difficult to approve totally of the young person your child is dating. Perhaps such-and-such a girl that your son is dating is "too wild." The boy your daughter is going out with is unreliable; you wonder whether you can trust him to drive while sober; you wonder just how much pressure he is putting on your daughter to have sex with him, etc., etc.

Even if your worse fears about the person your child is going out with are well-founded, it is very difficult to "forbid" your child to see the other person. (It's not difficult to do the forbidding, but it's difficult to make it stand.) In these circumstances, my advice is to be courteous to any person whom your child brings to the house. Courtesy is a form of respect not only to your child's date, but it is a form of respect to the judgment of your child, which is important in building up a trusting relationship between you.

If, however, dating rules that have been firmly established are broken, then you clearly have a right to impose limitations on the relationship. In doing so, it may be possible to open a discussion about how your child views the person he or she is dating. Maybe you can find out what's behind the attraction, and depending on the degree of respect and trust between you and your child, you may be able to state openly the concerns that you have about the person being dated. If you go about this not in an accusatory manner, but, rather, as one who is simply curious as to "how things are going," you may find out that your child shares many of your own concerns, and really isn't all that interested in the other person; or, possibly, you may find out that some of your own fears are *unfounded*, that your kid has shown better judgment in dating this particular person than you had at first realized. At least, you should be open to this possibility, and try to see in the other person what your child sees.

The Child Who Doesn't Want to Date

Some teen-agers give the appearance of being ready to date, but show little or no interest in members of the opposite sex. Physical development is not necessarily an accurate indication of a corresponding psychic development. Some teen-agers are just not ready to date, for a variety of reasons—shyness certainly being one reason high up on the list. It takes a lot of courage for some kids to risk exposure of all their secret fears about themselves by stepping into the dating arena for the first time. (Any reader who has been divorced, and suddenly has been put in the position of going out and meeting new dating friends will understand easily this reluctance on the part of teen-agers.) A case of acne, even a pimple or two, to a teen-ager can seem like the most hideous disfigurement. Girls who believe their breasts are too small (or too large); boys who are concerned about the size of their biceps, or chests, or penises, or whatever—all may be reluctant to expose themselves to the ridicule which they are certain awaits them the minute they attempt to start dating.

It is understandable why teen-agers should have these fears. The world showers them with its stereotypical images of what constitutes romantic desirability. It is a rare child, indeed, who will sally forth with confidence into a world in which he/she risks offending as a result of bad breath, pimples, greasy (or non-greasy) hair, ragged nails, menstrual stains, bulging tummy, drooping breasts, or near-sightedness. I can only advise parents to be patient and understanding with teen-agers who are reluctant to date. Perhaps a bit of reassurance can help. Would it reassure them to know that *you* yourself once begged out of a date because of a particularly ripe raspberry pimple that was blossoming on the end of your nose?

The teen-ager, of course, who does not measure up to stereotypical standards of beauty may have a real problem when it comes to dating. There are kids who are cross-eyed, pigeon-toed, whose teeth could use straightening, who have facial or other scars, a speech impediment, a learning disability, a hearing defect, a limb deformity, a limp. Such kids may have a tough time for a while—until the time when a fuller maturity arrives. It may take a bit longer for the kid with one or more physical or other defects to find a sexual partner. But the time will arrive. Let your kid know this. Let your kid know that real love which is the basis for the best sex is based on a great deal more than just physical appearance. The time will come, too, for such a kid.

What If Your Kid Is Homosexual

Before anything else, it should be made clear that a teen-age boy or girl who is shy, or who does not date, or who shows behavior mannerisms normally associated with the opposite sex (for example, "limp wrist" in boys, "mannish" behavior on the part of girls) is *not necessarily homosexual.* For a parent to confront such a child and accuse him/her of being homosexual would be a heinous act difficult to forgive.

Even in instances where sexual contact has taken place between teen-agers of the same sex (both boys and girls), it does not necessarily indicate an orientation to adult homosexual preference. Particularly in circumstances where members of the same sex are isolated from the opposite sex, as in certain sex segregated schools, for example, there can be a certain amount of homo-erotic activity that is distinct from a committed homosexual orientation and preference. It used to be said that the entire British ruling class at one time or another, and to one extent or another, had taken part in homo-erotic activities in sex-segregated boarding schools. Homo-erotic behavior for these boys of privilege was a temporary outlet for sexual desires in the absence of female partners. In Alfred Kinsey's classic report on male sexual practices*, it was revealed that 37 percent of all males in the U.S. at one time or another had participated in a homosexual encounter *to the point of orgasm.* Thus, merely "doing it" on an experimental basis—particularly in our sexually

*Kinsey, A. C., Pomeroy, W. B. and Martin, C. E. *Sexual Behavior in the Human Male.* Philadelphia: W. B. Saunders, 1948. p. 623.

liberated culture—is not an indication of homosexuality.

I have raised this matter of the non-homosexual teen-ager who exhibits "homosexual mannerisms" or who has participated in limited homo-erotic encounters because there is so much confusion about the subject of homosexuality today. I have had teenage boys burst into tears and "confess" to me that they were "homosexuals," when, in fact, they were thoroughly heterosexual, but were categorizing themselves as homosexual because of society's notions of how homosexuals behave and what homosexuals do, how heterosexuals are supposed to behave. The point is that one should be very cautious about categorizing a teen-ager as homosexual on the basis of superficial evidence.

On the other hand, we do know that homosexuality exists, and because increasing numbers of homosexuals feel free to state openly their sexual preference, we know that they exist in relatively large numbers.

If you should learn that your son or daughter is homosexual—either because he/she tells you, or because it becomes clear as a result of obvious sexual signals over a long period of time—very likely the realization will come to you as something of a shock. There are parents who react by wanting to banish their own children from their sight. Other parents will take on feelings of "guilt," and blame themselves for what they consider a terrible affliction.

Certainly it is not easy to be homosexual in today's world. Even in our "liberated" times, homosexuals have it tough, don't kid yourself. If they do not currently feel guilt and self-loathing, we know from abundant evidence that at the very least they have gone through periods of experiencing such feelings. Additionally, there exists the problem for homosexuals of facing into a world of great hostility against homosexuality (homophobia) on the part of much of the heterosexual (straight) world.

Aside from these very real difficulties, however, it may be comforting to parents of teen-age homosexuals to know that most mental health professions today do not consider homosexuality an *affliction* or illness. That's the good news. Homosexuality is seen as an *alternative lifestyle*.

The bad news for many parents is that whatever the underlying reasons for a homosexual orientation are, if your teen-ager is homosexual, it will do absolutely no good whatsoever for you to try to talk him or her out of it. If you try to do this, you will succeed mostly in driving a wedge between yourself and your youngster. Whatever the underlying basis for homosexuality is, it is a complicated matter, and family homilies are not going to change the reality. The best thing that you can do if your child is homosexual is to acknowledge the reality of it, and not make your youngster's life harder than it already is by criticizing, or blaming or trying to change what, in fact, exists. The homosexual youngster has a right to love, and to be loved, as much as the heterosexual youngster. If your teen-ager is homosexual, my advice is to give him all your love; he probably needs your love now more than ever.

What About "Strange Crushes"?

As I have said, during the teen-age years un-formed youngsters are casting about for role models to help them develop a better understanding of themselves. In Problem #7 ("My Kid Doesn't Have Any Friends") there is reference to the matter of close exclusive attachments between two individuals of the same age, oftentimes of the same sex, but not necessarily so. In these exclusive relationships, teen-agers rely on one another for social and psychological support, and they look to one another for guidance in the development of their own individual personalities.

Teen-agers also look to older persons, sometimes of the same sex and sometimes of the opposite sex, for guidance and role patterning. If a teen-ager finds an older person who seems to represent all that the youngster looks up to and values in life, admiration of the older person can easily develop into a dependence—having all the aspects of sexually motivated affection. The teen-ager can't seem to get enough of the older person, whether it be a teacher, a coach, a next-door neighbor, a relative, it could be anyone.

"Mr. So-and-so says this," and "Mr. So-and-so says that." The child is quoting Mr. So-and-so to a degree that can make parents want to strangle Mr. So-and-so.

Don't do it—at least, don't do it until you have looked into the matter more carefully. Chances are Mr. So-and-so or Miss Whosis really are upstanding and outstanding role models for your kids, and it is good for kids to look up to them, and try to pattern themselves, to some extent, after them. Obviously, an obsessional interest on the part of a teen-ager toward an older person should be looked into to make sure that the child is not being exploited in any way—either sexually or any other way. There can also be the case of a teen-ager who has developed unrealistic romantic feelings which will interfere drastically with other areas in his or her life. In most cases, however, these teen-age "crushes" are normal, and healthy, and the intensity of feeling doesn't last much more than a few months.

What About Pornography and Masturbation?

For a teen-ager, there is no escaping a persistent sexual drive. Not only is the sex drive unrelenting, it has no proper sense of timing. Recently I had a muscular 16-year-old male gym instructor of two- to 12-year-old girl campers describe to me his humiliation when he developed an erection while leading a class through routines in front of their parents. His embarrassment became particularly acute when one little three-year-old grabbed the "handle" to steady herself after having stood on her head.

For teen-age boys and girls alike, the most obvious and immediate outlet for relief of sexual tension is through the means of masturbation. *Let's be thankful for this.* There was a time (not so long ago, either) when all kinds of maladies, including pimples, blindness, even madness, were attributed to masturbation. We know that these old shibboleths are no longer true; still, there is some concern on the part of parents lest their children masturbate to "excess."

Leave them alone. Let them do it. Masturbation is *natural*. It is a release from tensions that interfere with other activities that are important in their lives, too. If your son locks himself in the bathroom frequently, and you suspect that he is masturbating, *don't worry about it*. If you have an urge to go to the toilet, use the other bathroom. Or hold it. Or go behind a bush. Your son will be out in a few minutes, looking slightly dazed and calmed, and possibly sheepish.

Teen-agers, particularly boys, are stimulated by explicit sexual pictorial matter. (Also by written material and by sound tapes.) The degree of the explicitness in these media is not really important. Whether your kid is looking at close-ups of vaginas in some sleaze "sex" magazine, or ladies in Bloomingdale's silk underwear and lounge pajamas in a slick "family magazine," the result is the same, and my opinion is that, from a teen-age boy's point of view, it really doesn't make much difference. Chances are he picked up the family magazine from the living room coffee table; he picked up the "sex" magazine from the bottom of Dad's desk.

Magazines that attempt to stimulate sexual fantasies through the use of *sado-masochism*, violence against either men or women, or that portray sex in some of its more esoteric and "kinky" forms probably should be discouraged. They are about as harmful, in my opinion, as some of the "kinkier" and more violent programs we see on television—not much more, and not much less—which also should be discouraged. *Both* distort the true human content of sexuality, and contribute to adding confusion to a teen-ager's conception of sexual relations.

It may be unrealistic to think that you can *forbid*

a child to look at this kind of distorted sexual material. Since sexual activity, including masturbation, is largely a private matter, kids will find ways of looking at whatever they want to look at to get their erotic "kicks." It could very well be that it's just something that fell into your youngster's hands from a peer, and means nothing more than that. If so, have patience, it will soon disintegrate as a result of much use, and soon a new magazine will take its place. Chances are the new magazine will be one of Dad's, and the family will be able to feel reassured again.

What About Disease?

It would almost seem that somebody up there doesn't approve of sexual promiscuity among human beings. In the 18th century, the "pox" (the name at that time for *syphilis*) ravaged Europe. Syphilis is a progressive disease, and if unchecked, in its tertiary stage results in brain damage and madness and ultimately death. It remained incurable until well into the 20th century.

Less deadly, but excruciatingly painful, and sometimes culminating in closing off of the fallopian tubes and sterility in women and urinary tract blockage in men is gonorrhea. An effective cure for gonorrhea came along just in time for the sexual revolution to take place, at which time *herpes* became the new disease associated with hygenically unprotected sexual activity. There still is no cure for herpes, but new treatment does manage to control it during its active—and painful—phases.

Within the past four years, we have become aware

of a new dreaded sexually transmitted disease, *Acquired Immune Deficiency Syndrome*, or AIDS. Although much remains to be learned about AIDS, it is known that it is a virus transmitted through the exchange of body fluids—blood, semen, saliva, etc., and undermines the body's immunity to any number of diseases, sometimes several in combination. When this occurs, AIDS results in death. It is rampant among homosexuals who transmit it sexually and among drug addicts who transmit it by sharing infected hypodermic needles. Drug addicts apparently have managed to infect prostitutes who now are transmitting it to heterosexual males, who, in some instances, have transmitted it to non-prostitute heterosexual females.

A teen-age boy who might be persuaded by his peers to visit a prostitute as a "rite of passage" will run a high risk of contracting any one of the above-mentioned diseases. It would be tragic, indeed, if what was considered a one-time "sexual prank" were to result in contracting life-threatening AIDS. For a variety of sound health reasons, sexually active teen-agers should be forewarned to take hygienic precautions such as the use of a condom by the male.

A Few General Remarks

If it is a fact that everybody talks about sex, it is an ironic rule that hardly anybody talks about *his or her own sex habits*. It is particularly difficult for teen-agers to talk to their parents about their sex habits. Why? Because sex is the most personal and private of our many human activities, and when children reach puberty, it is one of their "rights" as individuals and as independent beings to put an end to the invasion of their privacy which has existed for the preceding dozen or more years, the whole of their life, in fact, up to that point. The days are over when you helped your little kids into their undershorts, or bathed them in the tub, or examined their rashes. They have eaten the apple in the Garden, and have lost their innocence; they know knowledge, and with knowledge has come the command to cover themselves.

So it is never easy for parents to talk to their teen-age kids about sex. Yet, there is no subject that needs talking about more. Whenever possible, I would advise discussion with teen-agers about sexual matters *prior* to sexual intercourse. Particularly steps that can be taken to avoid a pregnancy should be discussed (with both daughters and with sons), with the serious consequences of a pregnancy clearly laid out.

It is not easy to get into such a discussion with a teen-ager. I would say there are more "don'ts" to going about it than there are "do's." Whatever you do, *don't accuse* them of anything. Your objective is to open up a give-and-take discussion, not make them defend themselves. *Prying is a waste of time.* If they want to tell you what they're doing, they'll tell you; otherwise *asking* them won't get it out of them. They're likely to close up tighter than a clam in a typhoon. It's not to the point, anyway, whether or not they are actually "doing it." A better approach to the child might be *what if* you were to do it; are you aware of all that you need to be aware of? And is there anything you want to know that I can help you with?

Don't give them a big lecture. (Ho-hum and yawn.) It's a big turn-off. They can get a lecture in school. Just let them know that you understand, and that if there is anything they want to know, you are there to help them.

Chances are it's easier for a daughter to talk to her mother alone than to her father or even to her father and mother together. Same for a son. If he's going to open up at all, he's probably more likely to open up to Dad than to Mom.

Do try to be general. In other words, a mother might say to a daughter: "You and so-and-so seem like really good friends. If you ever want to talk about anything, you know I'm here to help." A father to a son: "You may find yourself getting pretty deeply involved with a girl one of these days. You probably know already how important it is to take certain precautions. If you ever want to talk about anything," etc., etc.

There is no guarantee that either of the above approaches will work. Your kid may say, "I know, Dad!" and then refuse to discuss anything further. But that's just for now. If you let your kid know that you are *available to talk*, a time may come when he/she will seek you out for some advice—hopefully, before any serious problems have developed.

If, after all, your kid should get into trouble— either your daughter, or your son—and they come to you finally for advice, or more likely at this stage for help, *don't turn away from them.* You may be disappointed in something that has happened; you may be angry, but no matter how badly you feel, remember, *it's the youngster who is in real trouble.* A pregnancy for an unwed teen-ager is a wrenching experience. It is not a time for finger pointing; it is a time for some clear thinking about the alternatives that exist and the various consequences of making a choice from among any one of them. It is a time when the family needs to come together—hopefully with both sexual partners involved, and even with both families of the sexual partners involved. If there is need for therapeutic counseling, or advice of clergy, it should be sought without hesitation.

Finally, let us try to raise our children to understand the all-important inter-relationship between sex and *love*. It has been said that the two most important things in human life are love and meaningful work activity. Unfortunately, we live in a time when too many people, I am afraid, confuse love with *aggressive sexuality*, and confuse meaningful work activity with *making money*.

Sex without love is a promise without fulfillment. Sex is *part* of love, but as one 16-year-old boy said to me recently, "Sex ain't everything. There's gotta be *something else*." It reminded me of the lyrics to one of my favorite Cole Porter songs. When the words first come at you, they make you laugh, because they seem to refer exclusively to everybody's favorite subject: sex. But the real *feeling of uplift* comes when you sing out the punch-line ending.

"Birds do it,
Bees do it,
Even educated fleas do it.
Let's do it! . . .
Let's *fall in love*!"

For Professional Assistance

In almost every community in the United States there are professional health facilities that parents of teenagers can turn to if they seek outside assistance.

Generally, help can be found in the Yellow Pages (or Blue Government Pages) of the phone book. My advice is to look under both sections.

Categories to search under include:

(in the Yellow Pages)
Marriage, Family, Child & Individual Counselors
Physicians & Surgeons
Psychologists
(in the Blue Pages)

Mental Health Dept. (State or Municipal)

Health Services Department (State or Municipal)

Education Department, look for "Guidance" or "Social Services" or "Social Worker" (Municipal)

Schools, look for "Guidance" (Municipal)

If you are unsuccessful in finding what you are looking for, simply call your child's school, and ask to speak to the Guidance Counselor.

A list* of Mental Health Facilities located in 29 densely populated cities follows. These facilities should be able to refer you to a qualified person who can provide professional help.

Atlanta, Georgia

Atlanta Counseling Center
714 Georgetown Square
Atlanta, Ga. 30341
(404) 458-6156

Child Service & Family Counseling Center
1105 W. Peachtree St. N.E.
Atlanta, Ga. 30309
(404) 873-6916

Child Service & Family Counseling Center
1471 Gordon St. SW
Atlanta, GA 30310
(404) 755-1510

---

*List compiled from *Directory of Mental Health Facilities and Services: A Guide to Adult Outpatient Mental Health Facilities and Services throughout the U.S.*, Ellen G. Detlefsen, Editor, Andrea Pedolsky, Managing Editor. John Wiley & Sons, New York, Chichester, Brisbane, Toronto, 1980.

Fulton County Health Dept.
Division of Mental Health
99 Butler St. SE
Atlanta, GA 30303
(404) 572-2961

West Mental Health Center
3703 Bakers Ferry Rd. SW
Atlanta, GA 30331
(404) 691-9627
(404) 572-2626 (Hotline)

Baltimore, Maryland

Baltimore Pastoral Counseling Service
N. Charles & Belvedere
Baltimore, MD 21210
(301) 433-2241

Family & Children's Society
204 W. Lanvale St.
Baltimore, MD 21217
(301) 669-9000

Northwestern Community Mental Health Center
3517-A Langrehr Rd.
Baltimore, MD 21207
(301) 922-0105

Boston, Massachusetts

Jewish Family & Children's Service
31 New Charden St.
Boston, MA 02114
(617) 227-6641

Judge Baker Guidance Center
295 Longwood Ave.
Boston, MA 02115
(617) 232-8390

Massachusetts Mental Health Ctr.
74 Fenwood Rd.
Boston, MA 02115
(617) 734-1300

Northend Community Health Center
332 Hanover St.
Boston, MA 02113
(617) 749-9570

Danielsen Pastoral Counseling Ctr.
745 Commonwealth Ave.
Boston, MA 02215
(617) 468-3475

Charlotte, North Carolina

Family & Children's Service
301 S. Brevard St.
Charlotte, N.C. 28202
(704) 332-9034

Mecklenburg County Mental Health Center
501 Billingsley Rd.
Charlotte, NC 28211
(704) 374-2191

Chicago, Illinois

Cabrini-Green Family Center
407 W. Division
Chicago, IL 60610
(312) 751-4490

Cook County Hospital
Dept. of Psychiatry
1825 W. Harrison
Chicago, IL 60612
(312) 633-6660

De Paul University
Community Mental Health Clinic
2219 N. Kenmore Ave.
Chicago, IL 60614
(312) 321-7879

Jewish Family & Community Service
1 S. Franklin St.
Chicago, IL 60606
(312) 346-6700

United Charities of Chicago
64 E. Jackson Blvd.
Chicago, IL 60604
(312) 939-5930

Cincinnati, Ohio

Family Service of the Cincinnati Area
2343 Auburn Ave.
Cincinnati, OH 45219
(513) 381-6300

Heinold Crisis Intervention Center
3301 Beckman Ave.
Cincinnati, OH 45225
(513) 542-6017

Jewish Family Service
1710 Section Rd.
Cincinnati, OH 45237
(513) 351-3680

Columbus, Ohio

Family Counseling & Crittenton Services
199 S. Fifth Ave.
Columbus, OH 43215
(614) 221-7608

Jewish Family Service
1175 College Ave.
Columbus, OH 43209
(614) 231-1890

Ohio State University Counseling & Consultation
  Services
Ohio Union, 1739 N. High St.
Columbus, OH 43210
(614) 422-5766

Worthington Community Counseling Service
5884 N. High St.
Columbus, OH 43285
(614) 888-8468

Denver, Colorado

Barnum Outpost/Centro De Las Familias
205 Knox Ct.
Denver, CO 80219
(303) 934-8942

Eastside Neighborhood Health Center
529 29th St.
Denver, CO 80205
(303) 892-1241

Westside Neighborhood Health Center
990 Federal Blvd.
Denver, CO 80204
(303) 292-9690

Human Services
1555 Xavier St.
Denver, CO 80204
(303) 825-3283

Dallas, Texas

Dallas County Mental Health Center
721 S. Peak St.
Dallas, TX 75223
(214) 826-2170

District V Community Mental Health Center
5925 Maple Ave., Suite 220
Dallas, TX 75235
(214) 943-5151

Pastoral Counseling & Education Center
2727 Oaklawn
Dallas, TX 75219
(214) 522-1590

Detroit, Michigan

Family Service of Detroit & Wayne County
51 W. Warren Ave.
Detroit, MI 48201
(313) 833-3733

Lutheran Social Services
484 E. Grand Blvd.
Detroit, MI 48207
(313) 579-0333

SouthWest Detroit Community Mental Health Service
1700 Waterman
Detroit, MI 48209
(303) 895-3838

Hartford, Connecticut

Catholic Family Services
896 Asylum Ave.
Hartford, CT 06105
(203) 522-8241

Family Service Society
36 Trumbull St.
Hartford, CT 06103
(203) 278-9374

Houston, Texas

Family Service Center
3635 W. Dallas
Houston, TX 77019
(713) 524-3881

Jewish Family Service
4131 S. Braeswood
Houston, TX 77025
(713) 667-9336

Indianapolis, Indiana

Catholic Social Services
623 E. North St.
Indianapolis, IN 46204
(317) 632-9401

Christian Counseling Services/Turtle Creek Medical
   Center
528 Turtle Creek N. Dr.—Suite E 1
Indianapolis, IN 46227
(317) 783-6604

Jewish Family & Children's Services
1717 W. 86 St.—Suite E
Indianapolis, IN 46260
(317) 255-6641

Kansas City, Missouri

Counseling Institute
411 Nichols Rd.—Suite 246
Kansas City, MO 64112
(816) 931-9580

Jewish Family & Children's Services
1115 E. 65 St.
Kansas City, MO 64131
(816) 333-1172

Midwest Christian Counseling Ctr.
605 W. 47 St.
Kansas City, MO 64112
(816) 561-3726

University of Missouri/Kansas University Counseling
  Center
5319 Rockhill Rd.
Kansas City, MO 64110
(816) 276-1000

Memphis, Tennessee

Memphis State University
Center for Student Development
111 Scates Hall
Memphis, TN 38152
(901) 454-2291

NorthEast Community Mental Health Center
5515 Shelby Oaks Dr.
Memphis, TN 38134
(901) 381-3880

Los Angeles, California

Airpost Marina Counseling Service
6228 W. Manchester Ave.
Los Angeles, CA 90045
(213) 670-1410

California Community Service Ctr.
8380 Melrose Ave.
Los Angeles, CA 90069
(213) 653-2173

Chinatown Services Center
600 N. Broadway
Los Angeles, CA 90012
(213) 680-4288

East Los Angeles Mental Health Service
512 S. Indiana St.
Los Angeles, CA 90063

Hammel House
4340 Hammel St.
Los Angeles, CA 90029
(213) 268-9161

Kedren Community Mental Health Center
7760 S. Central Ave.
Los Angeles, CA 90001
(213) 777-1411

Los Angeles Jewish Family Service
6505 Wilshire Blvd.
Los Angeles, CA 90048
(213) 852-1234

The Mental Health Clinic of Westwood United Meth-
   odist Church
10497 Wilshire Blvd.
Los Angeles, CA 90024
(213) 474-3501

South Central Mental Health Service
1313 W. 8th St.—Suite 320
Los Angeles, CA 90017
(213) 483-6192

South East Mental Health Services/Hubert Humphrey
  Satellite
5850 Main St.
Los Angeles, CA 90003

Volunteers of America
Family Counseling Service
5300 Monica
Los Angeles, CA 90029
(213) 462-7186

West Central Mental Health Service
3751 Stocker St.
Los Angeles, CA 90008
(213) 299-3680

Miami, Florida

Jewish Family & Children's Service
1790 SW 27 Ave.
Miami, FL 33145
(305) 445-0555

Scott Family Health Care
5601 NW 27 Ave.
Miami, FL 33142
(305) 635-7701

United Family & Children's Services
18861 S. Dixie Hwy.
Miami, FL 33157
(305) 232-1610
(305) 643-5700

Miami Mental Health Center
2121 SW 27 Ave.
Miami, FL 33145
(305) 547-6162
(305) 446-3311

Milwaukee, Wisconsin

Family Service of Milwaukee
2819 W. Highland Blvd.
Milwaukee, WI 53208
(414) 342-4558
(414) 963-1444-Hotline

Jewish Family & Children's Services
1360 N. Prospect Ave.
Milwaukee, WI 53202
(414) 273-6515

Lutheran Social Services
3200 W. Highland Blvd.
Milwaukee, WI 53208
(414) 342-7175

Milwaukee Area Technical College Counseling Center
1036 N. Eighth St.
Milwaukee, WI 53203
(414) 278-6233

North Shore Counseling Service
5906 N. Port Washington Rd.
Milwaukee, WI 53217
(414) 332-8280

St. Michael Hospital Mental Health Center
2400 W. Villard Ave.
Milwaukee, WI 53209
(414) 263-8000

Springdale Community Mental Health Clinic
7411 W. Cold Spring Rd.
Milwaukee, WI 54220
(414) 321-2400
(414) 257-7402

Minneapolis, Minnesota

Family & Children's Service
414 S. Eighth St.
Minneapolis, MN 55404
(612) 340-7444

Jewish Family & Children's Service
811 La Salle Ct.
Minneapolis, MN 55402
(612) 338-8771

Pilot City Mental Health Center
1349 Penn Ave. N
Minneapolis, MN 55411
(612) 348-4622

New Haven, Connecticut

Catholic Family Services
478 Orange St.
New Haven, CT 06502
(203) 787-2207

Connecticut Mental Health Center
34 Park St.
New Haven, CT 06508
(203) 772-3300

Family Counseling Of Greater New Haven
1 State St.
New Haven, CT 06511
(203) 865-1125

Jewish Family Service of New Haven
152 Temple St.
New Haven, CT 06510
(203) 856-1125

Pastoral Center/Hospital of St. Raphael
(203) 789-3000

New York, N.Y.

Nathan W. Ackerman Family Institute
149 E. 78 St.
N.Y., NY 10021
(212) 879-4900

Catholic Charities Family & Children's Service
34 W. 134 St.
N.Y., NY 10037
(212) 281-9320

Family Service Association of America
44 E. 23 St.
N.Y., NY 10010
(212) 674-6100

Jewish Board of Family & Children's Services
120 W. 57 St.
N.Y., NY 10019
(212) 582-9100

James Weldon Johnson Family & Children's Counsel-
    ing Ctr.
2089 Third Ave.
N.Y., NY 10027
(212) 860-7284,85,86

Lower Eastside Service Center
Mental Health Clinic
46 E. Broadway
N.Y., NY 10002
(212) 431-4610

Lutheran Community Services
33 Worth St.
N.Y., NY 10013
(212) 431-7470

Puerto Rican Family Institute
116 W. 14 St.
N.Y., NY 10011
(212) 924-6320

Volunteers of America
340 W. 85 St.
N.Y., NY
(212) 787-1212

Philadelphia, Pa.

B'nai B'rith Career & Counseling Services
1405 Locust St.
Philadelphia, PA 19107
(215) 545-1455

CATCH
130 S. Ninth St.
Philadelphia, PA 19106
(215) 928-7659

Counseling & Guidance Clinic
222 N. 17 St.
Philadelphia, PA 19103
(215) 735-3323

Family Service of Philadelphia
5700 N. Broad St.
Philadelphia, PA 19141
(215) 549-8600

Family Service of Philadelphia/North East District Office
(215) 744-4700
South & West District Offices
(215) 735-7900

Jewish Family Service of Philadelphia
1610 Spruce St.
Philadelphia, PA 19103
(215) 545-3290

La Salle College Counseling Ctr.
20th St. & Olney Ave.
Philadelphia, PA 19141
(215) 951-1355

Pittsburgh, Pa.

SouthEastern Clinic/South Hills Health System
Outpatient Services
4127 Brownsville Rd.
Pittsburgh, PA 15227
(412) 881-2255

Adult & Adolescent Clinic/Psychoanalytic Center
211 N. Whitfield St.
Pittsburgh, PA 15206
(412) 661-2300

Portland, Oregon

Delaunay Mental Health Center
5215 N. Lombard
Portland, OR 97203
(503) 285-9871

Multnomah County Mental Health Division
426 SW Stark, 7th Floor
Portland, OR 97204
(503) 248-3619

Tualatin Valley Mental Health Center
14600 NW Cornell Rd.
Portland, OR 97229
(503) 645-3580

Rochester, N.Y.

The De Paul Clinic
681 Brown St.
Rochester, NY 14611
(716) 436-4840

Family Service of Rochester
31 Gibbs St.
Rochester, NY 14604
(716) 232-1840

Monroe County Mental Health Clinic for Sociolegal
    Services
99 Exchange St.
Rochester, NY 14614
(716) 454-7200

St. Louis, Missouri

Malcolm Bliss Mental Health Center
1420 Grattan St.
St. Louis, MO 63104
(314) 241-7600

Catholic Family Service/St. Louis
8039 Watson Rd.
St. Louis, MO 63119
(314) 968-8012
(314) 371-4980 (at Lindell Blvd.)

Family & Children's Services of Greater St. Louis
2650 Olive St.
St. Louis, MO 63103
(314) 371-6500

Grace Hill Neighborhood Health Center of Consolidated Neighborhood Services
2500 Hadley St.
St. Louis, MO 63106
(314) 241-2200

Jewish Family & Children's Service
9385 Olive Bldg.
St. Louis, MO 63132
(314) 993-1000

Magdala Foundation
1129 Penrose Ave.
St. Louis, MO 62107
(314) 652-6004

San Francisco, California

Family Developmental Center
3045 Santiago St.
San Francisco, CA 94116
(415) 661-7274

Family Service Agency of San Francisco
1010 Gough St.
San Francisco, CA 94109
(415) 474-7317

Mission Mental Health Center
1665 Mission St.
San Francisco, CA 94103
(415) 558-2564
(415) 558-2507 (West)

SouthEast Mental Health Center
4190 Mission St.
San Francisco, CA 94112
(415) 595-7753

Way Home Community Counseling Centers/San Francisco
1666 Lombard St.
San Francisco, CA 94123
(415) 928-0595

Seattle, Washington

Applied Psychological Services
4558 17 Ave.
Seattle, WA 98105
(206) 525-1250

Catholic Social Service
1715 E. Cherry St.
Seattle, WA 98122
(206) 323-6336

Lutheran Social Services of Washington
19230 Forest Dr. NE
Seattle, WA 98155
(206) 365-2700

Pioneer Square Neighborhood Health Station
206 Third Ave. S
Seattle, WA 98104
(206) 624-6601

Presbyterian Counseling Service
1013 Eighth Ave.
Seattle, WA 98104
(206) 623-7090

Washington, D.C.

Howard University Counseling Service
Fourth St. & Howard Pl NW
Washington, DC 20059
(202) 636-6870

Pastoral Counseling & Consultation Centers of Greater
  Washington
3000 Connecticut Ave. NW
Washington, DC 20008
(202) 281-1870

Andromeda/Hispano Mental Health Center
1823 18th St. NW
Washington, DC 20009
Tel. & Hotline (202) 667-6766

District of Columbia Institute of Mental Hygiene
3000 Connecticut Ave. NW
Washington, DC 20008
(202) 462-5090

Index

About the Authors

DR. LAWRENCE BAUMAN is a senior clinical psychologist at Coney Island Hospital in New York, and an adjunct assistant professor at New York University. He is married and is in private practice, working extensively with teenage boys and girls.

ROBERT RICHE is a free-lance writer, a former United Press staff correspondent in New York, and a playwright. He is married and the father of a teenage son and a teenage daughter.

For parents who want to raise their children better...
and for the adults those children will become.